Alien in the Delta

Thankful Strother

ISBN- 13: 978-1479139026
ISBN- 10: 1479139025

DEDICATION

To my wife Barbara and my children Darnell
and Christine

CONTENTS

Acknowledgments

To my family and friends I appreciate your being in my life. Thank you for your encouragement and support throughout the writing of this book. The input and feedback that you provided was invaluable. Your ideas and suggestions were very helpful in the overall development of *Alien in the Delta*. I hope that you enjoy the book.

Author's Note

This book is a memoir.

Having been called many different names at various times in my life, I would like to explain how I became Thankful Strother. My first nickname was Thee. In Germany, it was Gerard, or Gary. After joining NCR Corporation, I was known as Ted, or Teddy. Now, I have decided to select my own first name.

Through research into my family's genealogy, I discovered that my great-great grandfather's first name was Thankful. In his honor and as a testimony to my life's experiences, therefore, I am Thankful Strother.

"The fountain of content must spring up in the mine, and he who hath so little knowledge of human nature as to seek happiness by changing anything but his own disposition, will waste his life in fruitless efforts and multiply the grief he proposes to remove."

Samuel Johnson

Chapter One

Beginnings

Grandfather shot the man as he opened the gate to the front yard. The man died on the spot. After killing the man, my grandfather went into hiding for seven years. This event was the legacy left to my father by his father. Would what happened thirty years before my birth have an impact on my life?

I was born in 1943 in a farmhouse at Grand Lake, Arkansas, the seventh and last child born to my mother. A midwife assisted with the delivery, which was customary during that time. My mother was forty years of age, and my father was forty-three at the time of my birth. They had five boys and two girls; one boy died before I was born. My name is Thankful Strother.

Before my first birthday, my parents bought a newly built house on an acre lot in the small town of Eudora, Arkansas. The white-wood house had a tin roof and a large front porch that ran the width of the house.

It had three rooms, a living room with a fireplace, a kitchen, and a bedroom. We had electric lights when most families used kerosene lamps. We did not have indoor plumbing; we had an outhouse. The screened front porch was to keep out mosquitoes and flies. A swing on the porch hung from the ceiling and could comfortably seat two people. Our family got a lot of pleasure from the use of that swing. We had a corner lot, with the house facing east at Front and Arch Streets. Our enclosed lot had a five-feet-high galvanized-steel-wire fencing separated into three sections: a yard for the house, a place for the chickens and pigs, and a garden. The largest section of the lot was the garden, where we grew vegetables including tomatoes, greens, beans, sweet potatoes, okra, squash, and peas. We grew and raised most of our food. My father was very proud of the house and lot because we owned it free and clear without any debt. This was where I grew up.

Four of us lived in the house; my parents, my sister Vicky, and me. The four older siblings had already left home. I slept in the same room as my parents, and my sister, Vicky, slept in the living room. When she was fourteen she had a baby girl. Vicky was sent away to live with my brothers up north after she had the baby so that she could try to start her life over again, without a child. My mother said that Vicky had been a great disappointment to them. Our parents were ashamed and embarrassed, and they felt responsible for my sister's pregnancy. I am only four years older than my niece, Lynn. We grew up together, and Lynn was like my little sister. My parents raised her to adulthood.

The unpaved street that we lived on was without gravel. In the summer heat, when the temperature was around ninety degrees, it would be covered with a layer of powder-like soft dirt. As cars passed, the dirt would fly up and leave behind a dust cloud that would take several minutes to settle. When it rained, the street became very slippery and unsafe to drive on. It was like driving on a sheet of ice. A few cars would always get stuck in the mud or slide off the street into a ditch.

In back of our house, there was a juke joint that was always noisy on the weekends. Loud blues music played on the jukebox late into the night. Sometimes, I would hear gunfire. Drunks would get into fights, using profanity and yelling so loud that it would awaken me. By the age of seven, I had heard most of the profane words. The activities that took place in the dark outside the juke joint, late into the night, were things that a seven-year-old boy was not supposed to see. But it was exciting to watch. Not knowing what to expect next was frightening and entertaining at the same time. I continued to look, until my father caught me and told me to get back into bed.

When the noise would get very loud, my father would go to the juke joint and ask the owner to please keep the noise and language down because he was trying to raise a family. I was always afraid that my father would be harmed and not return home. But no harm ever came to him.

My hometown was in the southeast corner of Arkansas near the Mississippi River. Work in the area was seasonal and dependent on the cotton growers. The only full-time jobs were working at the saw mill or in the cotton fields. Our town had two cotton gins and a cotton-compress factory. School was closed at twelve noon in September so that children could help pick cotton. I went to the cotton field a few times with my mother, but my father objected. I am very grateful to him for finding someplace else for me to work. The people in our small community cared for the well-being of each other and shared a family like closeness. We showed respect for our elders by addressing them as Mr. and Mrs. and using Sir and Ma'am. The church was very important to the community, and most people attended every Sunday. When someone died, the ringing of the church bell let the community know.

Even though I loved the people in my community, I disliked intensely almost everything about where I grew up. I always felt out of place.

My Parents

Martilla Barnett Strother, my mother, was born in 1903. Her mother died when she was fourteen, so she helped to raise her younger brother and sister. She completed just three years of school, and the rest of her education was obtained through experience and hard work. She was a seamstress who took in sewing for people in our community to make a little extra money. Some of her customers would ask to pay her on an installment plan, and she would tell them to pay when they could. While working in the cotton fields of Arkansas, Mississippi, and Louisiana, she raised six children. When I was six years old, she was still working as a housekeeper and babysitter.

My mother was a strong believer in God. I didn't share a similar belief at age fifteen and that disappointed her. My mother spent a lot of time praying for me to become a believer. She would hold my hands as she spoke with me about God. She would tell me that God loved me and that I should have faith in him. But it did not matter how much I wanted to please my mother by telling her that I believed and had faith in God, I just couldn't lie to her. I will always treasurer those talks with my mother about God.

After my father died in 1972, my mother lived alone, but she was never really alone.

Whenever I went home to Arkansas, she always had people of all ages coming to visit her. She became a substitute parent for many young people who lived nearby. Her favorite topic was God, and her favorite activity was raising and feeding her chickens. Whenever we talked on the phone, as long as she discussed those chickens, I knew everything was going well.

One day we were talking on the phone, and she told me that she had sold her chickens. I knew immediately that something was wrong. I called my brothers and sisters and told them what has happen. This was not good news. Those chickens were like her children. She died six months later in February 1990, at the age of eighty-seven.

Edward Strother, my father was born in 1900 also had three years of schooling. Three years of school was good back then, because only six years of school at that time was offered. When I was growing up, most people in our community over the age of forty could

THORN CREEK NATURE CENTER

247 Monee Road, Park Forest, IL 60466

708-747-6320   thorn_creek@att.net

Visit our Website - tcwoods.org

Nature Center Closed:

Friday, Nov. 25 & Sunday, Nov. 27 - Thanksgiving
Friday, December 23 & Sunday, December 25—Christmas
Friday, December 30 & Sunday, January 1 —New Year's

Nature Center open Friday and Sunday, noon to 4p.m. Closed Saturday.

Trails open daily year-round, dawn to dusk

Thorn Creek Woods Nature Preserve is comprised of 985 acres of oak-hickory woodland, dotted with vernal ponds and dissected by Thorn Creek and its tributary streams. Over 3 1/2 miles of trails meander through woodland, floodplain forest, scenic ravines and pine plantations. Trails lead to marshy Owl Lake and a wetland swpl

FALL-WINTER

September 2016 - February 2017

not read or write. People would bring their personal letters and business documents to my father so that he could read and check them. He would respond to the letters and documents on their behalf.

My father was the secretary and treasurer of his church. That job required him to take and keep minutes of all church meetings and to retain accurate records of all financial transactions. He was very knowledgeable with his limited formal schooling.

In terms of their competence, he and my mother were educated far beyond three years of school. My father would often say that he wished opportunities were available when he was younger to get a better education. I believe he would have been very successful if given that opportunity.

I learned many things from my parents, but what has sustained me throughout my life is that children should respect, honor, and obey their parents. Also tell the truth and stay away from trouble when possible. Those teachings have served me well.

My Grandparents

John Strother, "Papa," was born in 1876, and Lillie Strother, "Grandma," was born in 1880. They married in 1898 and had four children who lived into adulthood: three girls and one boy. My paternal grandparents had more children, but they all died at childbirth.

When I was in the second grade, my grandparents built a white two-room house with a tin roof and located it about 150 feet to the right of our house, in what had been our garden. We still had a large enough garden remaining to share with my grandparents. After they moved next door, I saw them daily. I would go to their house every day to eat because Grandma was a great cook and always prepared enough food for both families. My mother was not a very good cook. I believe this was because we always lived close to my grandparents, so my mother never had to cook.

But she made one thing better than anyone else, and that was her yeast rolls and bread. They were the best!

I consider myself very fortunate to have had my grandparents living near by while I was growing up. My grandfather was a great storyteller. We all had favorite stories that we liked to hear him tell. It did not take much persuasion to get him started on a story. He used to tell us that he was one of the first people in the town to own a Model T Ford. Sometimes, when he was drinking liquor, he would try to drive his Model T home and would forget that he was driving a car. In his drunken state, he would think he was in a horse-driven wagon, and would yell out, "Whoa" to get the car to stop. Most of the time, the car ran off the road or into something. Luckily, Papa was never hurt.

Papa had what he described as horrible nightmares. My very favorite story was about what caused his nightmares. When Papa was a young man, he killed a man and before being captured went on the run for seven years. The dead man would come for Papa nightly. He must have relived that shooting hundreds of times in his dreams. Grandma would have to awaken him to stop his screaming.

Papa went to prison for two years and seven months, and he served most of that time as a prisoner who was put in charge of guarding fellow prisoners. Papa would not only tell this story, he would stand up and show everyone exactly how it happened.

This is what I remember about the story. Papa was inside his house when this man came to the front gate and called him to come outside. Papa must have expected trouble because he went to his front porch with a Colt

.45 in his hand, and he asked the man to leave and not to come on his property. But the man wouldn't leave. In fact, he told Papa that he was going to come inside the yard and kick his ass. Papa warned him that if he opened that gate, he would shoot him. The man ignored Papa and opened the gate, and Papa proceeded to empty his gun into him.

Papa would then stand up and pretend he had a gun in his hand to show how he shot the man. That's when my grandma would say.

"John, why are you telling that child about that man you killed?"

My grandmother had lost her hearing, so she didn't know what papa was talking about until he stood up and pretended he had a gun in his hand. Papa never told us who the man was or why he was threatening our family.

Papa was not convicted of murder, but he went to prison for leaving the scene. That's why his prison stay was so short. After he served his time, a permanent job was offered to him as a prison guard, but he returned home to his family.

Papa stopped believing in banks after losing twenty-five hundred dollars during the Great Depression of the 1930s. When Papa went the bank to withdraw his money it was closed and out of business. After that, he started to keep his money in Prince Albert tobacco cans, which he would bury around his house. Sometimes, he would forget where he buried the cans and would spend the day digging up the yard, looking for his money. There are probably some cans filled with gold coins and bills still buried around his house. What do you think?

Aunt Sarah Bell

Aunt Sarah Bell lived with my grandparents, in much the same conditions as we lived, except they did not have electric lights in their house. They lived in what is known as a shotgun house, with two rooms. The front room served as the living room and bedroom. The back room was the kitchen and bedroom. It had a small front porch. Instead of owning, my grandparents lived in a rented house before they built a new house next to our house.

My father's youngest sister, Sarah Bell was an adult who acted like a child. I am not sure if she was born that way or if something happened to her at an early age. She was always happy and playful around me. I could tell that there was something different about her because she didn't act like any other adult I knew. I don't remember when she became ill, but she wasn't ill very long. One day she was alive, and the next day she was dead. She was only thirty-seven when she died. This was the first death that I had experienced. I felt sadness that I had never felt before, and it made my heart ache. The coffin was brought with Sarah's body to my grandparent's house and left there for two days. People came to the house throughout the day to view her body. My mother told me to sit in the room with the coffin to show my respect. I stayed in the room and greeted people as they viewed her body. This was very traumatic for me, at age seven, to stay and watch the reactions of family members and friends. The crying made me feel so much pain inside my heart. I wondered if that sad and hurt feeling would ever go away.

School Years

My years of school from first through sixth grades are all a blur, except for a few situations that I still remember. One of my earliest recollections was about something that happened to me at recess when I was in the first grade. I wanted to ride on the merry-go-round, but I was too small to get on the seat without someone lifting me up and placing me there. After someone put me on the ride, I was told to hold tight because the merry-go-round would be going very fast. I held on with one hand, and in the other hand I held a handkerchief, where my mother had tied up fifteen cents for me to buy my lunch. As the merry-go-round speeded up, I held on with all my strength, but it wasn't enough to keep me from being thrown to the ground. When I got up, I no longer had my handkerchief. I had lost my lunch money, and I began to cry. When I told my teacher what had happened, she gave me lunch money. The next recess I didn't go near the merry-go-round I went on the slide!

In the first grade, we took a nap every day around 1:30 p.m. We were told to keep our heads down on the desk, but I was so excited around other children that I could not resist raising my head to see what was going on around me. The teacher caught me looking and punished me by making me stand in the corner for five minutes with my face to the wall. This was the first time I received disciplined at school.

Be Quiet

I do not remember anything about the second and third grades, but in the fourth grade, I sat in the front row where I could see everything. Our teacher told everyone to stay quiet, and then she left the classroom. I proceeded to talk. I was the only one who seemed to want to talk, so I asked why everyone was so quite. No one said anything, so I turned around, and the teacher was right behind me. I have no idea how she returned to the classroom without me seeing her. After I got caught, her appearance so startled me that I stopped talking in class for a very long time. Do you see a pattern developing? I talked a lot at a young age. Talking became very important in my future career.

Corporal Punishment

We had our first male teacher when I was in the fifth grade. He really did not make much of an impression on me, except that he was a horrible teacher. I'm sure I did not learn one single thing that year in his class. It was very disappointing. The boys were all afraid of him because he used a dark-brown leather strap that was about four inches wide and three feet long to whoop any boy who got out of line. The girls in his class were not included in the whooping. He had that leather strap made just for whopping boys. Let the beatings begin!

My most memorable educator was my sixth-grade teacher, Mrs. Pride, who had taught for over forty years. She had taught many of our parents. She was very well-known and respected. One of the best teachers in the school, she demanded respect and had no problem hitting you with a cane stalk. I got hit a couple of times for talking. She would hit you on the hand or across the shoulders and the legs. The cane stalks were hard and dry like bamboo. Your hand would swell up when struck and turn red. Today, she would go to jail for the treatment we were given.

Summer Vacations

I visited my mother's sister, Aunt Victreen and her husband Uncle Rufus, in Little Rock, Arkansas, during the summer when I was eleven years old. They had a bathroom with a large bathtub. I would fill the bathtub with water and try to swim in it. Noticing this, Uncle Rufus took me to a community swimming pool, where he was going to teach me how to swim. We did not talk about his teaching methods before we arrived at the pool. Once we were at poolside, I asked him what I should do. He said.

"Just jump in and swim."

That was one of the most irresponsible things that an adult could tell a child to do. I almost drowned, and to this day, I am afraid of the water, and I do not know how to swim, thanks in part to Uncle Rufus.

The next summer, when I was twelve years old, my parents arranged for me to visit my grandfather's brother, Uncle Sylvester and sisters' Aunt Rebecca and Cornelia, in Chicago. Uncle Sylvester was a barber and had his own barbershop on Maxwell Street, in what was then called "Jew Town." All types of merchants from every country filled Maxwell Street. You could find anything that you needed or wanted. People from all over Chicago would come to Maxwell Street to shop. The street seemed to never end, as continuous stands were set up along the way to sell various merchandise. The smell of fresh food filled the air. Maxwell Street was such a wonderful and exciting place for me to visit. I looked forward everyday with anticipation wondering what new experience was in my future for that day.

Aunt Rebecca prepared lunch for uncle Sylvester daily, and one of my jobs was to take it to him and wait until he finished eating. While waiting, I had to sweep the barber shop floor. Then I would return home with the empty dishes from his lunch.

I had to take two buses on my way to and from Maxwell Street. At the bus stops and on the buses, young gang members robbed me several times. I was approach once by gang members with a police officer standing on the other side of the street. After being robbed, I told the police officer what had happen just minutes before. He didn't show any concern for my situation except to tell me to stay out of trouble. He treated me as if I had provoked the robbers.

The visit to Chicago was my first exposure to big-city life, where the doors were kept locked, and traffic sounds from the street were very loud and noisy. Stories about crime filled the newspaper daily.

I watched television for the first time in Chicago. I would sit for hours and watch anything that was on TV, even the cooking shows. That summer vacation exposed me to a lot of new thing including a visit to the Chicago zoo.

The one thing that stands out vivid in my memory was a visit to the Chicago Natural History Museum. I spent a whole day looking at prehistoric animal skeletons and playing with the exhibits. It was a wonderful place to go for a kid who had a curious and open mind. I wanted to buy something to remind me of my visit. The only thing that I could afford was a rock collection with twelve different small samples in a display case. I bought that rock collection and kept it all through high school. I believe we still have it someplace in storage.

Uncle Sylvester owned and lived in a two-family flat on the west side of Chicago on Trumbull Street, between Fourteenth and Fifteenth. Across the street lived the mother of Dinah Washington, the very famous Blues, and Jazz singer. Her two boys lived with their grandmother. The boys played outside, but they were never allowed to leave the yard. Dinah Washington came to visit her family while I was in Chicago. She arrived in a very large black limousine. Reporters filled the street. I didn't know who she was then, and I had no interest in seeing her. Looking back, I wish that, I had paid more attention to the events surrounding her visit to our street.

At the end of summer vacation, I returned home from Chicago with all kinds of wonderful stories to tell my friends.

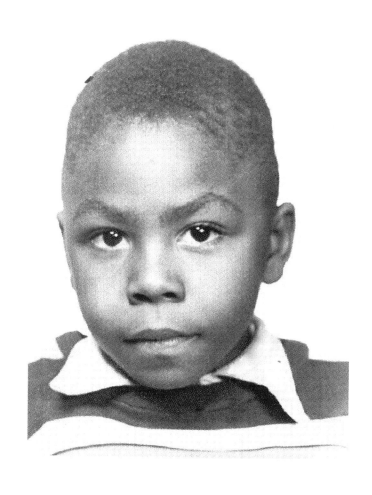

Here I am at six years old in 1949.

Chapter Two

Music

"Lonely Tear Drops," written by Berry Gordy and sung by Jackie Wilson, was the song playing on the record. Hearing that song at age fourteen made me feel that I had never really listened to music. That one song changed my way of thinking about music forever. Prior to that, the only music that I had heard was blues, country, and gospel, and I didn't like any of it. This new music made a lasting impression on me. My friend's mother had just purchased the new recording. As we listened, she danced with her son a few minutes and then left us alone. Because there were no girls at my friend's house, we paired up and danced with each other. Our attempt at dancing exposed the truth, which was that neither of us could dance. Creating our own personal dance moves looked stupid and pathetic. I thought dancing would come naturally. We realized that we didn't know what we were doing, but hearing that song made me want to dance. The next step was to find someone to teach me how to dance, since I enjoyed the music so much.

Most of the girls my age already knew how to dance. I asked my cousin Ozora to teach me how to slow dance. After an hour of my stepping on her toes, she said I was ready for the dance floor. But I wasn't satisfied with just slow dancing. I wanted to learn how to swing dance. Recruited for this task was my neighbor. She was a year older than me and well-known for her dancing ability. She took me on as her student, and in one day I learned the basics of swing dancing. It was now left up to me to keep improving and develop my style. Dancing became my passion. I would dance when possible. It wasn't long before I became a respectable dancer, and I can still slow dance.

Thumbs Up!

My junior high school experiences began in a new building with air conditioning. This made such a difference when the temperature soared to ninety degrees. My teacher, Miss Smith, was very young and petite. She could have easily been mistaken for one of her seventh-grade students. The most noticeable thing about her was that her right hand had only one finger, a thumb. I don't recall anyone ever asking her how she lost the other four fingers. She had a way of holding a piece of chalk with her right thumb while writing on the chalkboard. Do you understand why that impressed me so much? Try holding chalk with only your thumb. That takes superhuman strength.

When we had school dances, we could dance with our teachers. I was always a little reluctant to swing dance with Miss Smith because I had to hold on to that strong right thumb as we danced. Funny, the things you remember about people. Thumbs up!

Mary

At the end of the school year, I returned to Chicago for another wonderful summer vacation. I lived with the same uncle and aunt whom I visited the previous year. My duties were still the same: take lunch to my uncle every day, sweep the barbershop floor, wash the shop windows, and run errands. It wasn't long before word got out that a new kid was on the block, and other teenagers began to stop by to visit with me.

A fourteen-year-old school dropout named Jessie somehow became my friend, and he would visit me every day. I soon found out why the regular visits; it was because he had made arrangements to meet with a girl who lived just four houses from our house. Her name was Mary, and she was thirteen years old. Her father was a local well-known boxer.

All of the boys were afraid to talk to Mary in his presence. Jessie asked me to relay a message to Mary because her father would not allow her to talk to him. I called Mary one day to relay Jessie's message, but her father picked up the phone and asked who was speaking. I identified myself, and he told me to never call his house again. Now, I was really afraid of Mary's father because he knew my name and where I lived.

I was sitting on the stoop in front of our house when Mary's little brother told me that his father wanted to talk to me about Mary. Horrified, I went anyway. He asked me to come in and take a seat. Sweat dripping from my head and face, I told him I was okay standing. That way, if I had to run out of the house, it wouldn't take me too much time to get away. He asked me again to sit down next to him on the sofa. So I sat down. He asked me if I liked his daughter. I said yes, and then he called Mary and asked her to come in and sit on his other side. He asked her if she liked me, and she said yes. What came next was unexpected and surprising.

He wanted to know if I was available on Saturday to go on a picnic with him and his family. I said yes, I would be happy to go with them. He warned me about my friend, Jessie, telling me that Jessie was a dangerous young hoodlum and that I should stay away from him. Well, I went on that picnic, and guess what happened? That's right, Jessie showed up at the picnic! Mary's father told him that he wasn't invited and asked him to leave. Jessie left reluctantly. I enjoyed the rest of the day with Mary and her family.

After the picnic, Mary's father said that I was welcome at his house and could come by anytime. It was a good thing that I was leaving Chicago soon because Jessie was very angry with me. He came by the house everyday asking for me. I stayed in the house until it was time to leave Chicago. I was so glad that I made it back home to Arkansas without having to face Jessie.

I had stories to tell my eighth-grade class about my summer vacation. When asked what happened on my vacation, I would tell them that, I stayed alive.

Puppy Love

The next school year went by quickly, when summer came; I did not go away that year.

My cousin told me that a cute girl living near his house wanted to meet me. He took me to her house and introduced me. I really didn't know what to talk to her about, so my cousin did most of the talking for me. He mistook my silence for a lack of interest in the girl. He asked if she knew other girls whom she could introduce me too. She had a friend who wanted to meet some boys. The girl she talked about had attended a different school but was transferring to our school in the coming school year.

Soon after that meeting, my cousin gave me a note from the new girl. The note expressed her wish to meet me. I wanted to answer her note, but not having much experience writing notes, I went to my older girl cousin for help with composing a letter. In my reply, I thanked the girl for the note and expressed my wish to meet her as well. We lived in a very small community but, our homes were about five miles apart, and we didn't have a telephone at our house. We began corresponding through the mail. The post office was two miles from my house. You had to pick up your mail from the post office because we didn't have mailman in our town. We wrote to each other almost every day throughout the summer. Getting a letter from her was such a thrill for me. Sometimes, I would go to the post office twice a day expecting a letter from her.

We wrote passionate letters filled with

words about loving each other even though we had never met. We both wanted to see each other in person, so eventually we set a date, time, and place to meet. The day of the meeting, I took a bath, wore my best jeans and shirt, and tried to look my very best. My palms began sweating hours before our meeting. The excitement and anticipation were almost unbearable. I had never seen her before; she told me that she would be wearing a blue dress. We planned to meet Saturday afternoon at the downtown post office. I waited in the post office for about fifteen minutes before a girl wearing this beautiful blue summer dress came through the door. When we finally met, we held hands and walked to the drug store for ice cream. This was my very first recollection of trying to impress a girl. We spent that afternoon talking and getting to know each other better. After our first meeting, I was so excited to rush back home and write her a new letter. The letters were as romantic as thirteen-year-olds could write. During that summer, it was a pleasure walking to the post office, knowing that her letter would be there, expressing her love for me. She was my first girlfriend and my first exposure to the feeling of being in love with a girl, even if it was only puppy love. I wish I had kept those letters.

First Job

The only jobs available in the summer were in the cotton fields. My father did not want me to pick cotton, but my mother said I had to do something, so I went to the cotton fields with her a few times. We had to get up at 5:00 a.m. We were in the field by 6:00 a.m., and we picked cotton all day. If you picked one hundred pounds of cotton, you would be paid two dollars for the day. That summer I earned ten dollars picking cotton, and my lunches cost me five dollars, so my net earnings were five dollars for the summer. I learned that manual labor was hard work and not for me.

My father came home one day after school started in the fall, and told me that he had found me a job working for the Eudora Enterprise Newspaper, and that I was to report to my job immediately. So I went to work after school that same day. I met the owner he explained my duties to me: wash windows, sweep the floors, take out the trash, dust the furniture, pick up lunch, and deliver papers or documents. The owner said that if I had an interest in learning how to operating the printing press he would teach me. But I would have to stay after my work ended and that I would not be paid extra wages. So I stayed after work to learn how to run the printing press.

The newspaper was prepared for printing once a week. The printing press used very large sheets of paper that were fed through the press on both sides, and then the sheets went through a machine that folded and cut the paper into eight sections to complete the process.

Eventually, the owner gave me the responsibility for running the printing press and folding machine. My job expanded into something more than just cleaning and washing windows. It became kind of a semi-skilled job. I was asked to find a replacement for my other duties. All of this started when I was fourteen years old. I worked after school for the newspaper every week until I graduated from high school.

Exotic Beauty

A lot of new and wonderful things began to take place in my life at the age of fourteen. I became interested in girls, developed an appreciation for music, and learned how to dance. Something else very nice was about to happen.

An exotic, beautiful girl with long, black, wavy hair came to Arkansas with my cousin's mother from up north. She had been dating my cousin but he didn't come with them. She lived up north all of her life and had never traveled to the South. It was not safe for her to travel in the South with her mother and father. She was a child from a mixed marriage; her mother was black, and her father was Italian.

She was staying at my cousin Ozora's house. One evening, Ozora brought her to my house and asked if I would go dancing with them. Word had gotten out that she would be at the dance club. The girl from up north was the talk of the town among the boys. After we arrived at the club, she became the center of attention. She demonstrated to us how the kids danced up north, and we showed her how we danced in the South. All of the boys wanted to dance with her, and she danced with everyone who asked her to dance. We all watched her dance to the music, making moves that we had never seen or imagined anyone doing while dancing. She was having fun embarrassing all the boys who danced with her. The club closed early, and we went to another place to dance. This time, I finally got up enough courage to ask her to slow dance with me. We danced closely together for a long time with her head pressed up against my face. My eye became red from her hair being next to my face. I was the only person slow dancing with her the rest of the night.

We went to my house after leaving the dance club and sat in the swing on the front porch. I asked her why my cousin had not come with them. She said that my cousin had cheated on her, and they had a fight. But she still planned to marry him when they turned seventeen. We were about the same age, but she was so much more mature than me.

The night we went dancing, she was determined to get even with my cousin for cheating on her. She said I was nothing like my cousin and that she would never forget me. She asked me not to forget her. While asking me not to forget her, she began to French kiss me. I had never been French kissed. What a surprise! What a pleasant surprise! WOW! She was returning up north the next morning, so we continued French kissing late into the night. How could I ever forget her?

The next time I saw her, she was seventeen, pregnant, and married to my cousin. They divorced three years later.

Sex Education

Several of my teachers in junior high school were young women who had just finished 'teachers' training. Ours was the first class they had taught for a full school year. The young teachers were about six years older than their students.

Sex was a frequent topic of discussion with our young teachers. Are you still a virgin? Have you ever had sex? Do you enjoy sex? Do you use protection? How often do you and your girlfriend have sex? The young female teachers asked the boys these types of questions. All of the boys thought it was cool having this kind of personal relationship with our young female teachers. Some of the young women teachers gave private sex lessons to the more mature male students. I was not advanced or mature enough to be given lessons, but we had lots of personal contact and inappropriate discussions with our young female teachers.

Was what we did with our teachers wrong or harmful? I don't believe that I suffered any emotional or psychological harm because of the inappropriate behavior of our young female teachers. However, I am in therapy.

Bull

We began taking shop classes my freshmen year in high school. We took shop for four years. A four-year project was a requirement to graduate. Our project was to raise a male calf to a bull, which would be displayed and judged every year at the county fair. The object was to win a blue ribbon. We also had to join the 4-H and Future Farmers of America clubs. Both of these organizations required that you build something to display at the county fair. In addition to the class project, I built a three-shelf corner "what-not stand" that could be used to display figurines. I received a white ribbon at the county fair for my efforts.

Another requirement was to learn and demonstrate how to use parliamentary procedure. Each school in the county put together a parliamentary-procedure team, and once a year, we would have a contest to determine which team was the best in the county. The best team in the county would compete in a statewide contest. The year we competed, our team came in second place out of nine teams.

At the time I wondered when and if, I would ever have an opportunity to use this knowledge. Looking back, I can say that I have used most of the knowledge I gained in high school shop, with the exception of not having raised a male calf to a full-grown bull. Maybe that's still in my future.

Runaway Child

It was at the beginning of my tenth-grade school year that I noticed a beautiful girl in the seventh-grade. She would smile at me every time we made eye contact. I didn't respond to her obvious flirting. One day, I could no longer resist her smile and we begin talking. The conversation was about our age and grade difference. We were attracted to each other, but we both knew that our friendship was leading no place for now. She agreed that I was too old for her and told me to wait a few years until she was a little older, and then we would date. I told her that she was going to break hearts when she grew up.

She lived with her grandmother, who was well acquainted with my mother, and they would often talk. The grandmother expressed concern about her granddaughter not listening and obeying her anymore. She told my mother that her granddaughter had threatened to run away with her boyfriend and live with his family. My mother asked me to stop by the grandmother's home to see if I could be of any help.

I spoke with my young friend, trying to find out what was happening. The grandmother thought she was too young to date. But she had already been seeing a boy who her grandmother didn't approve of because he had dropped out of school. She said her grandmother was too strict, and sometimes she wanted to run away. I pleaded with her not to run away from her home. Then she promised me that she wouldn't run away.

Noticing that she hadn't been coming to school, I asked some of her classmates if they had seen her. They told me that she had dropped out of school and run away from home. I wasn't surprised.

Several months later, I had forgotten about her. When on my jobs at the newspaper, I received a call from the hospital. Everyone at my work was concerned that someone in my family was sick or had been injured. I got on the phone, the person on the other end wanted to know if she had Thankful on the phone. I said yes, and she said that she was calling from the hospital because a young woman's wanted to let me know that she had just had a baby boy, and she wanted to name her baby after me. Who had a baby? She wanted to do what? What was the young woman name? I was told it was my young friend who had run away. The hospital clerk wanted to verify the correct spelling of my name. I hesitated and took a deep breath. This was such a surprise and a lot to process quickly. What if I wanted to use that name for my child? Would people think this was my baby? What would my parents think? Why me? Those were just a few thoughts that went through my mind. I finally told the nurse that she had spelled my name correctly. I then asked how the young lady and the baby were doing. The nurse said okay. I told her to extend my congratulations to my young friend and the father.

When I got off the phone, my boss wanted to know if everything was okay, and I told him that this young woman had named her baby boy after me. Everyone at my work found out about the child with my name. I was teased for at least a week. Can you believe that anyone would want to name her child after me? I didn't tell my family about what had happened because I didn't want to try explaining the reason. After that call from the hospital, I never heard anything about or from the young woman and the child again. I have often wondered where that child with my name is now.

Self-aware

In the tenth grade, our English teacher, Miss Benton introduced us to some of the classics of literature. Books we may never have picked up on our own. Trying to interpret and grasp the meaning of some of these books was very challenging for me. But the more I read, the more I enjoyed them. I developed an interest in reading books during that class. Miss Benton really cared about her 'students' education. I can truly say that I learned more in her class than any of my other classes in high school. Miss Benton was one of my favorite teachers because she was always exposing us to new things.

Most of my classmates had never seen or heard of a tape recorder. Miss Benton brought one to our classroom and recorded our voices individually. Then she assembled our class and asked us to listen and identify the voices on the tape. We had difficulty recognizing some of our classmate's voices. When they got to my voice, it seemed like my entire class yelled out in unison, "That's Thankful!" I had never heard my voice before that day. It was a real big surprise to me that all my classmates recognized my voice. Before hearing myself speak on the tape, I thought we all sounded the same when we spoke. My voice sounded so different from my classmates, which confirmed my belief that I was an alien in the wrong environment. It was the first time I realized there was something different about me. This was a very important growth step for me. I knew that, at some point in time, we all feel we are different from others. This was my beginning of becoming self-aware. The year was 1959, and I was fifteen years old.

Green Tongue

I wasn't very athletic in school, but I was active with the basketball team as an assistant manager. My job was to keep track of the basketballs, the team fouls, and the scores. I sat next to the coach during the games and cheered the loudest. This gave me the opportunity to travel out-of-town with the team. I went to all the games without having to pay. This was my first taste of freedom.

One night, the basketball teams played out-of-town at a high school, which was thirty miles from where we lived. After the girls basketball teams finished their game, a very tall girl with light gray-blue eyes from the rival girls basketball team came over to me and said.

Hey, boy, what's your name"?

"Thankful." I said

"What do your friends call you? She asked.

"My friends call me Thee," I said.

"I don't like that name." "From now on, I'll call you my boyfriend." She said.

She was one of the most popular girls in her school and played on the 'girls' basketball team. When she said that she wanted to be my girlfriend, and I said okay.

This was a great confidence builder for me because she chose me, was two years older than me and a senior in high school. She had been dating seniors, and now she chose me, and I was just a sophomore. We only saw each other at basketball games or other school activities.

Our high school basketball teams played the district championship games in her home town. We stayed in that town as long as our team won. This gave me a chance to visit my girlfriend at her home. She asked me to come over to her house at about 5:00 p.m. because her parents would not be home. When I arrived, she invited me in, and we sat on the sofa and began kissing. We French kissed for a long time. By now I was very proficient at French kissing. When we kissed, I tasted liquor on her lips. Stopping to catch my breath, I noticed that her tongue was green. I wondered if my tongue had turned green also. Was this some new kissing technique I hadn't heard about, one that turns your tongue green? After making a quick assessment of the situation, I remembered how surprised and displeased I was, seeing her green tongue and smelling the alcohol on her breath. She asked me to have a drink of crème de menthe (a mint-flavored alcoholic beverage) with her, and when I refused, she told me to leave her house. I got up to leave, but she wouldn't let me go and held on to my shirt. Finally letting go of my shirt, she asked me not to leave. I realized that she was tipsy. So I left the house anyway, and I never saw her again. However, she sent me her picture and an invitation to her graduation ceremony. She had planned to attend college in the fall. Thinking back on that situation, I would enjoy having some crème de menthe on the rocks now.

After my last encounter, I was a little apprehensive about getting involved with another girl. But I soon recovered with the help of a friend who was a very smart girl. She was younger than me and not as intimidating as my last girlfriend. We often studied together, and we were good buddies. Eventually, we decided that we would try being girlfriend and boyfriend. What a different kind of relationship we had together. There 'wasn't any fire or passion in this relationship. We remained friends, but we stopped dating after a few months. Sometimes, it's just better to have a friend who is a girl.

Juvenile Delinquent

I was in the eleventh grade when the fellows whom I hung around with tried to get me to do things that I had been taught were wrong. Those three fellows were my best friends. They drank beer, wine, and whiskey, and they kept trying to get me to join them. I always came up with some excuse not to participate, and most of the time, they left me alone. But one night after basketball practice, one of them had a cheap bottle of wine, and we all had to take a drink from the same bottle and pledge our everlasting friendship and loyalty to one another. This time, I could not escape. So I took just one drink and was about to leave when one of them suggested that we break into the school cafeteria and steal whatever we could carry. They told me that I had made a pledge, and I couldn't chicken out on them now. We found a window that had been left unlocked, and we climbed through it. Once inside, I began to get cold feet. I could visualize getting caught and going to jail, embarrassing my parents, never completing high school, and destroying my life. What do you think happened? Well, I stole whatever I could carry, and that was a box of twenty-four small cartons of milk. I took the box of milk home and asked my father if he wanted to buy it for $2.25. He said yes and wanted to know where I had gotten the milk and if I could bring home more tomorrow. I told him that I had gotten it from school, and I would try to bring home another box tomorrow. *No crime or lie ever goes undetected.*

The next day, my father wanted to know why I 'hadn't brought home more milk. I told him that the school sold out of extra milk. But he 'wasn't satisfied with my explanation. He visited the school and spoke to the person I said had given me the milk. He asked him about the milk that I had brought home. My father wanted to be put on a waiting list if the school ever had any more extra milk for sale.

The person who talked to my father came to me afterward and said.

"I know that you and your friends stole

from the school cafeteria. I will not report you, but I am disappointed in you. It would break your' parents' hearts if they ever found out what you have done. So stay out of trouble and get a new set of friends."

I can't drink milk today without getting sick. I guess that's my punishment.

State of Bliss

One night after a basketball game, I was walking home with other students, and in the group was a very cute girl. She was the younger sister of a girl who was in my class. We started to talk to each other. It was the first time we really had a conversation. I was surprised at how much I enjoyed talking with her during that short distance. When we reached my house, we said goodnight to each other, and she continued on toward her house, which was about four blocks away.

A feeling of excitement came all over me

that night as I thought about her again. The next day on our way home, we talked all the way to her house. A few more days passed before I asked her if I could carry her books. Asking a girl to carry her books meant that you had an interest in her, and if she allowed you to carry her books, she also had an interest in you. That was the first step in the courting processing.

I finally met her parents after carrying her books for a week. When you are young, everything takes such a long time. You are in a hurry to make things happen quickly. So we spent as much time as possible with each other, having lunch together and stopping to talk to each other when we passed in the hallway.

The next step was asking her if she would be my girlfriend. After she consented, lots of handholding and kissing took place. We began to show affection for each other, and how much we enjoyed being together. We were falling in love. The most exciting phase came next. That's touching each other in private places. I am sure you can guess what happened next. This wonderful relationship and state of bliss lasted throughout high school.

College Scholarship

The twelfth grade seemed to go by faster than the other grades. It was the easiest because it wouldn't be long before high school would be over forever. I had a steady girlfriend, a job, money, and freedom to stay out until midnight. I started to feel more like a man than a boy. I went dancing with my friends almost every night. We were just having lots of fun, but we still had to graduate.

In class, we discussed our future plans, deciding which college to attend or if we were even going to college. Preparing for graduation was time consuming. It was also expensive, spending money for pictures, a class ring, a cap, and a gown. Taking pictures, going to rehearsals, practicing marching, and delivering a speech kept me busy.

Day of commencement ceremony finally arrived, and I gave a speech, marched, and received my diploma, and school was over. I was seventeen years old and second in my class when I graduated from high school. I was offered a partial scholarship to Bishop College, a historical black college founded in Marshall, Texas, in 1881 later moving to Dallas, Texas. Bishop College closed in 1988.

I didn't accept the partial scholarship because my family wouldn't have enough money to cover the other college-related expenses. During that time, financial assistance was not so really available.

In my family, college was not strongly encouraged, and it was just assumed that I would do what my brothers had done and join the military. So that's what happened. Sometimes I wonder what my life would have been like today, if I had accepted that partial college scholarship. But things worked out okay anyway; I have no regrets.

High school graduation 1961 at age seventeen.

Chapter Three

The Air Force

Planning to join the US Air Force after graduating from high school was the one thing I had thought about for months before school ended in June of 1961. The US Air Force entrance test was scheduled for July in the Little Rock, Arkansas, recruitment center, where four branches of the US military services were located. On the day of the test, several hundred young men stood in lines to take the test to enter the military. We lined up by the branch of the service that we wanted to join and were led to a testing room and given instructions about the test. Then the actual test was placed on our desk with a pencil. We were given an hour to take the test, and upon completion it would be scored.

After completing the test, we waited another hour to get our results. We were called one at a time to talk with the recruiter. I waited with excitement for my name to be called. Upon hearing my name, I walked to the desk and sat down with the recruiter, expecting to hear how well I had done on the test, but instead the recruiter told me my test scores were not high enough to join the US Air Force. But the US Marines, Navy, or Army, would accept me with my scores. The recruiter said that, he would recommend me to any other branch of the services. I thought it over for about ten seconds and told the recruiter thanks for his recommendation but, I didn't have any interest in joining another branch of the military.

It was disappointing not passing the entrance test. Failing that test had destroyed all my future plans. My plan was to join the US Air Force the same as my brother, Curtis had done. He was in the US Air Force and I had admired my brother my whole life.

Curtis and his family had been stationed

in France for three years, and after returning to the United States, they came to visit us in Arkansas. I was twelve years old at the time and my four-year-old niece, Lei could speak French. It made such an impression on me that, I wanted to join the US Air Force, go to France someday and learn to speak French.

On the US Air Force application there were questions about being stationed overseas, when asked which foreign country you would like to live in. Of course, France had been my choice. Going to a foreign country and learning another language was going to be exciting, adventurous, and interesting.

After failing to be accepted into the US Air Force, my chances of living abroad seemed to have disappeared. My belief at the time was that my opportunity to go to France would never happen, and I was stuck in Arkansas forever.

However, my family rescued me from

the bleak future I thought fate had in store for me. A few months later, I was on my way to Detroit, where my brothers and sisters lived. When I got there, I went immediately to the US Air Force recruiter's office and took the test again, and this time my scores were good enough to be accepted into the US Air Force. I was seventeen years old, so I had to get permission from my parents to join the US Air Force. My parents signed the necessary documents, and I waited for my enlistment date.

Most of the time was spent with my sister, Vicky and brother, James. My brother was building a cabin sixty-five mile from Detroit in Rondeau Bay, Ontario, Canada. I helped him every weekend until it was time to leave for the US Air Force.

I was so anxious to go, and it seemed like such a long wait before being sent away to basic training. I would go to the 'recruiter's office every day to determine if he had heard anything about my enlistment date. I finally received the letter asking me to report for duty on December 5, 1961.

Basic Training

The recruiter sent six young men away together on the so-called buddy system. It guaranteed that we would remain together throughout basic training, which took place in San Antonio, Texas. If you have ever seen movies about basic training, then you know how we were treated. You start basic training the same day you arrive. All of your hair is cut off; your civilian clothes are taken away from you. You are given everything else that you will need from that point on, such as underwear, pants, shirts, shoes, socks, and so on.

Wake-up time was 5:45 a.m., and by 6:00 a.m., you were outside doing exercises. We had four squad leaders. Three of my buddies were made squad leaders. Each squad leader was responsible for twenty trainees. They helped to manage and train the men in their squad. When marching, they walked in front of their squad. I was selected as the right guard or flag barrier. That's the individual who stands out in front of the entire squad and carries the flag while marching. So my responsibility was to pay attention and listen for the commands from the drill sergeant. The squads would follow behind me as I carried the flag. To get us going, the drill sergeant would yell out, "SQUAD! FALL IN! ATTENTION! FORWARD MARCH!" To have the squad turn in a certain direction, he would yell, "SQUAD! RIGHT TURN MARCH!" To bring the squad to a stop, he would yell, "SQUAD! HALT! AT EASE!" Sometimes I made mistakes that were funny and embarrassing. For example, the drill sergeant would yell out, "SQUAD! HALT!" and I didn't always hear him, so I would keep marching until I had gotten about fifty feet ahead of the squad before noticing they'd stopped and that no one was marching behind me.

I would hear the sergeant say very loudly in the background.

"Let's see how far that idiot will go before recognizing that he's all alone."

Another embarrassing incident was when I marched straight ahead toward a building wall, not hearing the command to "HALT," "TURN RIGHT," or "TURN LEFT." I continued to march with the whole squad following behind me until I was directly in front of the building wall. The drill sergeant came up to me and said.

"Where are you going now? Who do you think you are? Superman? Go ahead; walk through the building wall, stupid."

Sometimes I would line up in formations without the flagpole.

"Strother, where is the damn flagpole? You have one job, and that job is to always have that flagpole with you."

"I didn't know where I left the flagpole." I said.

"Maybe if I stuck that flagpole up your ass, you would remember where to find it." He said.

Merry Christmas, Baby!

Basic training was the first time most of us had been away from home. We talked a lot about our families and girlfriends because we were all homesick. We knew the names of each other's girlfriends and wives. They became like members of our own family.

At the end of the day after mail call, we would share the good and bad news from the letters we had received. Some of the fellows began to receive "Dear John" letters after a few weeks. When that happened, we would gather around the guy to show support and talk about his ex-girlfriend as if she was the lowest person who lived on Earth.

I had bragged about my girlfriend being such a wonderful person and that we were planning to get married sometime in the future. It was around the Christmas holidays when I received a letter from my girlfriend. She wrote that she was no longer in love with me and that she was dating someone else. I was so hurt when I received my "Dear John" letter. But I had to accept that she had moved on with her life and that I should do the same. Merry Christmas, Baby!

Mixed Emotions

In the sixth week of basic training, two of us were sent over to the headquarters building. The captain wanted to let us know that we had been selected for overseas duty. This was great news. I had applied for France, and I was so excited. The captain called me in and said.

"I have your orders to go overseas."

"France?" I asked.

"No, you are going to Germany." The captain said.

The military would try to accommodate your request, but their requirements came first. A little disappointed that I wouldn't be going to France, I still looked forward to going to Europe.

With basic training done, six young men from Detroit headed back home on the train. Someplace in Texas, the train stopped so that we could stretch our legs and get a snack. The six of us got off the train and went into the restaurant to get something to eat. We were all dressed in our nice, new blue uniforms, proudly representing the United States Air Force. I walked into the restaurant with all my buddies, and before we could sit down, the waiter looked at me and the other black serviceman and said.

"We can't serve you in here. You have to go out back to order and pick up your food."

Born and raised in the South, I had experienced discrimination before, but this time it hurt me deeply because I was dressed in my US Air Force uniform and was prepared to die for our country, and yet my fellow countryman still wouldn't serve us.

This was the United States in 1962. No one should ever have to experience that kind of treatment! The both us just got back on the train without eating and sat in silence. We began basic training as six buddies from Detroit and returned as four white serviceman and two black servicemen.

Basic training in San Antonio, Texas 1962.

Germany Bound

After completing basic training, I had two weeks off before reporting for duty in Germany. A week was spent with my parents in Arkansas, and I spent the other week with my brothers and sisters up north. I then left for Germany with a stopover in Washington D.C. This was my first time in the capital, so I took a walking sightseeing tour and viewed several buildings and monuments.

The other hours waiting for the next train were spent in the United Service Organizations (USO) Center in the train station. Serviceman went there to relax, shoot some pool, or have something to eat. The next stop was Fort Dix in New Jersey, and from there we flew to Germany.

My very first plane ride was in a military C-118, which at that time was one of the largest planes in the military, old and large. The seats in the plane were all turned backward. The pilot was upfront, our backs were turned toward him, and there were no windows on the plane. I just sat there for hours listening to the various sounds the plane made. We stopped to refuel in Greenland. Then we flew into Rhein-Mein Air Force Base in Frankfurt, Germany. We arrived in February of 1962. Almost seventeen years earlier, the war with Germany had ended.

Willkommen

"Welcome to Germany," the plane's captain told us.

It had taken us eighteen hours, with one stop for fuel, to fly from New Jersey to Frankfurt. Buses were lined up near where our plane had parked to take us to various locations in Germany. We got on a military bus that had "Ramstein Air Force Base" written on the side. We left Rhein-Mein Air Force Base for Ramstein Air Force Base in Ramstein,

Germany, where I would be stationed. We drove about two hours before we arrived. The only things I knew about Germany were what I had seen in the movies. I expected a bunch of bombed-out buildings and cities. It was just the opposite. There were beautiful new buildings, highways (Autobahns), and streets. The countryside, with its rolling hills, was beautiful. The homes were all made of brick. Germans had gone through a war, but they were living so much better than the people in my home town.

The things I noticed right away were the different sounds of the language and how the Germans dressed. It looked like all the men worked in offices, because they were dressed in suits and ties and carried briefcases. I later discovered that they had their lunches inside the briefcases. My first impression of Germany was how clean, beautiful, and new everything looked. It was unbelievable to see how the Germans had recovered from the war.

The first person I saw after arriving on

base was my friend, who had been in basic training with me in Texas. It was nice to have him there to show me around the base. He took me to the barracks, where I got a room assigned to me. This room would be my home for the next four years. The barracks that we lived in housed everyone who had anything to do with transportation. The next morning at work, the new arrivals were asked to raise their hands if they could drive a vehicle. Just about everyone raised their hands except me.

Learning to Drive

What happened next was that we all went through driving school to learn the German road signs and traffic laws. Some of us who couldn't drive went to extra training to learn how to drive. Then we were taught to drive the smallest to the largest cars, trucks, tractor trailers, and so on. This took about three months. I had no interest in being a driver for four years and did everything in my power to get out of transportation, including damaging a few vehicles.

After three months of poor driving, an ultimatum was given to me, which was to learn how to drive or be transfer to a different department. To be transferred was exactly what I wanted to happen. What great news! An officer called me into the office one day and said.

"Since you cannot learn how to drive a vehicle, we are going to put you in the maintenance department."

The only people who were in maintenance were those airmen who had committed some sort of crime. Their duties were mowing grass, cleaning up, and picking up garbage. I did not understand why I was being punished, because the only thing I had done was not learn how to drive a vehicle. I had a week to learn how to drive or I would be transferred to maintenance. So I decided to start driving. They had no plans to put me in maintenance. This was just a tactic to get me to drive.

Job with Perks

The first vehicle I drove was a jeep to a US Army post about fifteen miles from the base. After my driving ability was discovered, I was assigned to an older airman who was being discharged from the military. My supervisor, a staff sergeant, asked me to ride with the older airman, learn from him, and prepare to take over his job. I rode with him for about a week to learn the job before he returned the United States.

His morning routine was to go to Ramstein Air Force Base Headquarters and pick up documents and deliver them to North Atlantic Treaty Organization (NATO) Headquarters (also on base). After that, he went to the south-side theater to pick up film canisters and deliver them to the north-side theater. He picked up film canisters from there and delivered them to the west-side theater. Then he took the film canisters from there and left the base to deliver them twenty miles away to the army post theater. From the army post theater he picked up the film canisters. The movies played at each theater for two nights and the routine started all over again. That task took two hours every other day to rotate the films.

He was finished with most of his tasks by noon every day. After lunch, he waited until 2:00 p.m. to go back to NATO Headquarters to pick up documents and deliver them to Ramstein Air Force Base Headquarters. He worked three hours in the morning every other day and one hour in the afternoon. That was his daily routine. When he returned to the United States, I took over his job.

What a great job! It came with additional perks that he hadn't told me about.

The theater managers would give me free passes to the movies because I delivered the films to each theater. Instead of turning in the pass each time and waiting to get another one, I had my pass laminated like a driver's license, making it a permanent movie pass. All of the theater managers got used to seeing my permanent pass and accepted it each time I went to the theater. I never had to pay to see movies on the air base in Germany.

What Time Is It?

I enrolled in college in the winter of 1962. I became a freshman on the US Air Force base in Germany, attending the University of Maryland extension campus. I started going to classes about two months after arriving at Ramstein. I took courses in history and English, getting my basic classes out of the way. One day while on a class break, a cleaning lady asked me what time it was in German. I didn't understand what she was saying. Then she walked up to me, took my arm, and looked at my watch. She thanked me and left. What happened made me feel very uncomfortable and a little stupid. It was at that moment I made the decision to learn to speak German. After finishing my history and English classes, I started taking German classes. I begin with basic German and ended up taking five different courses, as well as spending a lot of my free time studying German. I took speech-lab classes, using headphones with microphones that allowed a German teacher to monitor me.

I tried different avenues to learn to speak the language. I listened to German radio stations, not understanding a single word. I asked the Germans whom I worked with in the motor pool to help me pronounce words and to speak to me only in German. The German people were always willing to help with the language. Speaking German to the women in the laundry, which was on the first floor of the building where we lived, was a daily occurrence.

After drinking beer or booze and getting a little tipsy, I would only speak German. Drinking helped me to get rid of the fear of making a mistake. So the secret to learning how to speak another language is to move to that country, stay at lease two years, drink whatever booze the local people drink, get a little tipsy and start talking.

Chauffeur and Spy

Things went well on the job for about a year, until my supervisor asked me to provide him with a list of my daily duties. When it was discovered how little I worked all day, my job was eliminated. My duties were dispatched to other drivers.

I was assigned another job as a staff-car driver. The job required you to wear a dress blue uniform everyday. You look like an airman on a recruitment poster. Everything about this job was so formal, because you drove officers around from place to place. This was basically a chauffer's job. The officers would visit all of these obscure, top-secret missile sites all over Germany, and they were difficult to find. Some of the site locations were not identified on the map, and I would be given directions while driving to the site. That job didn't last very long because I got lost too often.

After being removed from that job, I was assigned another job working on the flight line. My duty was to provide transportation for the pilots. I drove them to their aircraft and picked the up from their aircraft.

The flight line was in a security zone, and you had to display your security badge at all times. One morning, after dropping off a pilot in the parking area, I went back on the flight line and began a conversation with one of my air-police buddies who was guarding aircraft. We were just talking about girls and football, having a pleasant conversation, and then he asked me to show him my security badge. Searching in my pockets and in the vehicle for my badge, I could not find it anyplace. After several minutes of looking for the badge, it was obvious I didn't have it with me. All of a sudden he blew his police whistle, and a vehicle loaded with air police came driving toward us at high speed with sirens blasting. Stopping in front of me, the air police jumped out of their vehicle, ordering me to lay on the ground with my hands behind my head. They put me in handcuffs and loaded me in the back of their vehicle. An air policeman sat in the back of the vehicle with me, pointing his weapon toward me as they drove me to air-police headquarters. After passing the security and background check, they determined that I 'wasn't a spy and released me.

It was unforgivable what they had done to me because we drank together every evening in the airman's club. Not being a stranger to them hadn't made any difference; I was still treated like a spy. Angry with those guys, I stopped speaking to them for the rest of my stay in Germany.

Woman and Baby in Danger

My next job was a temporary-duty (TDY) assignment to try to make some extra money. On that job, you were given money for your expenses, and it was always more money than you would use. At the end of the trip, you were expected to have a few extra bucks. The job was transporting top-secret materials to various military locations in Germany. On TDY, you would be away from the base at least three and sometimes four days.

I looked forward to the morning when I would begin my long trip. The vehicle was loaded overnight with classified materials. My destination was near Czechoslovakia, a long way away from Ramstein Air Force Base.

That first day I drove about halfway there. I stopped at a US Army post and slept overnight. The next morning I got up at 6:00 a.m., had breakfast, jumped into my vehicle, and was on my way. I had anticipated arriving at my next destination ahead of schedule. It was about 10:00 a.m., and I was making good time. The roads in Germany were very curvy and narrow, and I was probably going a bit too fast. I went down a hill, and it curved around a bend and up toward another hill, and when I got to the top of that hill, I lost control of the vehicle and was heading toward a tree. When I attempted to turn the steering wheel, the load shifted and made my vehicle lift away from the pavement. I couldn't hold on to the steering wheel any longer. It seemed to have a mind of its own, so I just let it go and put my hands on the seat to brace myself. A short distance in front of me, walking in the road, was a German woman pushing a baby stroller with a baby inside. Headed in the direction of the woman and baby, I held the steering wheel again trying to prevent an accident from taking place. I tried to change the direction of the vehicle, but it was out of control. I could feel the vehicle slowly turning over after sideswiping a tree.

Hanging upside down in the vehicle with my seatbelt attached, I begin to smell gasoline and heard dripping from the ruptured gas tank on the side of the vehicle. I panicked and couldn't get unattached because of my weight on the seatbelt. Finally getting my seatbelt off and falling to the inside roof of the vehicle's cabin, I was a bit disoriented because everything was upside down. Wanting to get out of the vehicle quickly, I made an attempt to kick the window out, almost breaking my leg. I must've seen too many movies thinking that would work. So then I rolled the window down, crawled out of the vehicle, stood up, and ran a short distance away from the upside-down vehicle. I noticed that the woman with the baby 'wasn't hurt, and a crowd of people had gathered. Walking toward the crowd, excited that I gotten out of the vehicle alive, I pulled out a packet of cigarettes, took a cigarette from the pack, and was about to light it when the crowd begin yelling.

"NOOOOO!"

They had noticed that I was covered in gasoline, and with the flick of my lighter I was about to blow all of us away. So they all were yelling.

"NEIN, NEIN, NEIN!"

Stopping me just in time, I yelled back to the crowd, "Danke schon" ("Thank you"). Soon after that, the police showed up, but they didn't arrest me. They took away my driver's license.

An investigation would take place to determine what happened and if I should be held responsible for the accident. I was grounded and assigned to the motor pool, washing vehicles, while the hearing was being conducted.

A month later the investigation was completed with a decision about what should happen to me. In Germany if you damage a tree, you must pay for the damage. The amount varies, depending on the age of the tree and the amount of damage it suffered. If the accident was your fault, the military made you pay for the tree and for the cost of repairing the vehicle. Money was taken from your pay every month until the items were paid off.

Upon completion of the investigation, I was found not guilty of any wrongdoing. Luckily for me, the German woman pushing the baby stroller told them that I drove up over the hill, saw them in the road, and in order to avoid hurting her and the baby, I flipped the truck over. I got a clean bill of health because of the German woman's testimony. It turned out that I was a hero for not hitting the woman and the baby.

She told them what she thought had happened. But honestly, I had no control over that vehicle; it had basically taken its own route and flipped over. After that, it was decided I would not be sent on any more temporary-duty trips.

I got another job assignment after that accident, working on the night-shift. The job was pretty much the same as before, except I would only go on shorter trips. The night-shift was great because you only worked two nights, and then you had one or two days off. I worked about four nights a week. That was a great shift, and I worked it until I left Germany.

My original tour of duty in Germany was for two years, and when it was up, I decided to extend my stay and spend two more years there instead of coming back to the United States. I continued to work the night-shift, delivering parts to various locations. I spent my entire service career in the US Air Force in Germany, almost four years with the exception of basic training, which was unusual for most servicemen because you normally had to transfer to someplace else after two years.

Kennedy Assassinated

When Kennedy was assassinated in 1963, I was at a basketball game on the base, and the game was interrupted. We were told to go back to the barracks. The entire base was put on stand-by alert after the announcement, waiting for more news about the president. Later on we found out that he had been assassinated. You can imagine the kind of things that went through our minds. We had just gone through the Cuban Missile Crisis in October of 1962 with the USSR. Our natural suspicion was to think that the Russians had something to do with the assassination.

We didn't know if we were going war. "This is it," I thought. "The end of my life, and I am so far away from home." Germany was the

United States' first line of defense. We were in imminent danger with Russia being so close to Germany. Do you know what it feels like to be frightened for a few minutes? Now try to imagine what that must feel like for a month. No one could leave the base until it was clear that we were not going to war with the Russians. It took at least six months before we began to feel like the world was not coming to an end.

Discovering Malcolm X

I began developing and discovering new ideas and values at the age of eighteen. I found out that some of the young men in my barracks would have group discussions about the various approaches to solving discrimination in the United States. I sat in on several discussions and began to follow the civil rights movement in the United States. The discrimination I had experienced in Texas was still fresh in my mind, and I became very interested in civil rights and the rights of black people in the United States.

When I joined the US Air Force in December of 1961, the eleven states that had been the Confederacy were still maintaining and practicing apartheid in the United States, the same as South Africa. My experience in Texas made me acutely aware that the US Air Force uniform and the pledge to die for the country had little or no meaning for a large portion of my fellow citizens.

I also discovered black authors and read books written by James Baldwin, Richard Wright, Chester Himes, and Langston Hughes.

I remember having a discussion about civil rights with a young white British citizen on the base. He asked me why were black serviceman in the military of a government that did not provide them equal rights. I said nothing. I didn't even attempt to answer the question. He then wanted to know what I thought about Malcolm X. Again I had no answer. That was the first time I had heard the name Malcolm X. Who was he?

I began asking other airmen if they had heard of Malcolm X. I was warned not to get involved with a group that had secret meetings, where they listened to his recordings and discussed his teachings and beliefs. Well, I found the leader of this group and asked if I could attend a meeting. He was very suspicious of me and told me he didn't think that it was for me. But I convinced him that I was really interested. He suggested that I read the autobiography of Malcolm X before I attended any meetings. He loaned me a copy of the book, and I begin reading. Most of the things I read shocked me because they were so radical and different from my way of thinking. I now understood why the meetings were kept secret. The leader of the group finally allowed me to attend a meeting.

In the one meeting I attended, we

listened to a recorded speech where Malcolm X advocated killing all the white devils if necessary. Having that type of material in your possession was just not allowed. It was a crime and considered subversive and anti-American. Before I had a chance to attend another meeting, the leader of the group was arrested.

During an annual inspection of the room where the group leader lived, all of the Malcolm X material was found in his locker and confiscated. The group leader was taken to jail, and a month later, he was court-martialed. He was found guilty of having questionable material in his possession; he was busted, reduced in rank, and lost his stripes and pay grade, but he was not discharged. He remained in Germany for another year. Before he left Germany, he met, fell in love with, and got married to a beautiful, blue-eyed white devil.

Martin Luther King received a lot of press, so I was somewhat familiar with his nonviolent efforts to gain equal rights for black citizens in the United States. Malcolm X was very controversial. He didn't believe in the nonviolent movement, which is what Martin Luther King practiced. At that time, I was more in the Malcolm X camp and not the Martin Luther King camp. I wasn't a separatist, but I was against American black men marrying German women.

I thought the men were being taken advantage of, because I believed the women just wanted to get a free ticket to the United States to become an American citizen.

I felt it would be a shame to marry a white woman instead of a black woman because of the racism that I had experienced at that particular time. I even went out of my way to discourage my friends who were interested in marrying German girls. I didn't think it was a good idea at the time, and my friend was dating a German girl.

When my friend told me that he was

getting married to his girlfriend, he asked me to meet her before I tried to discourage him. I went with him to a guesthouse in the city of Saarlouis and met his girlfriend. Her name was, Heidi, she was eighteen years old, very pretty, smart and spoke some English. My friend had already told her that I was against him marrying her. So our meeting was a little uncomfortable for me. I made an attempt to explain my reasons for objecting to the marriage, but all I did was show my prejudice. I don't' believe that I made a very good first impression on Heidi. However, several months later my friend and Heidi got married, and I was one of their witnesses.

After the wedding I began to rethink my position on marrying German girls. It wasn't long before I had changed my mind completely. What I realized was that my being against the marriage was based on my negative experiences with discrimination and race relations in the United States. Not every one shared my experiences or point of view. If I wanted to grow as a person I needed to have an open mind to new things and different situations.

Chapter Four

How I Met My Wife

An American serviceman had drowned in the Nied River, close to Saarlouis, Germany. He had been stationed at a US Army post near there. The body was brought to the medical facility at Ramstein Air Force Base for examination.

His sergeant came to the base to complete some paperwork before his body could be shipped back to the states. The sergeant brought with him several German girls who had known the young American. They lived in the area where he drowned and came to the base to show their respect.

I attended night classes at the University of Maryland three times a week. Classes ended at 8:00 p.m., and afterward I went to the airman club. When I entered the club, Jimmy, a friend of mine rushed up and asked me to go with him to a table where several German girls were sitting. Looking in the direction of the girls' table, I saw airmen crowded all around them. I told him that I wasn't going to the table with him.

"You don't understand. These girls don't speak or understand English, and I want you to interpret for me." He said.

He offered to pay for my drinks. I still refused.

"I don't believe that you can speak German anyway." He said.

Because of what he said, I felt the need to show him that I really could speak German. I said okay and went with him to the table. Sitting at the table was the sergeant from the US Army post along with four German girls. One of the girls was Barbara, who is now my wife. The other girls were Barbara's cousin Rosa and friends Karen and Heidrun. We all met that night and still remain friends.

The table was surrounded by guys all trying to talk to the girls. I began interpreting for Jimmy. After an hour, only a few guys were still standing around the table. When Jimmy ran out of money, he also left. I was getting ready to leave when one of the girls made me a proposition.

"If we bought your drinks, would you remain at the table?"

So I stayed at the table acting as the 'girls' interpreter. That's when I met Barbara for the first time. I saw Barbara several more times that year in the German town of Saarlouis, where she was with her friends at a guesthouse called the Mexico. This was a very popular place for young Germans to meet in a causal social setting. At some point, Barbara and I began to engage in conversation. I learned that she had a boyfriend, and he was in the German military. She worked as a hair stylist. After our conversation ended, I hoped to see her again. I liked talking to her and being around her, and I felt she liked me also. We wouldn't see each other again for almost a year.

Black Soldier

Ramstein Air Force Base was the largest air base outside of the United States. The base population was forty thousand airmen. There were over 250,000 servicemen in Germany; seventeen years after the war had ended. However, war was still fresh in people's minds. I came in contact with several Germans who had fought in the war and other people who had been in concentration camps. The young Germans were mostly from one-parent homes. Their fathers had been killed in the war. Most people my age had been children during the war and had suffered from food shortages and lack of shelter.

No sweets or candy were available during the war. Black soldiers would throw gum and candy to the children as they drove through the various German towns. The black soldiers had left a very good impression on some of the people.

Black soldiers were not allowed to fight on the ground in World War Two. They were relegated to service units, working as cargo handlers or cooks. Some Germans would come up to me crying or with tears in their eyes, remembering how well the black soldiers had treated them.

Some of my experiences in Germany seemed strange and unusual. I went to some villages where the children had never seen a black person.

In some German towns, people would actually encircle my black friends and me, staring and pointing at us as if we were from outer space. The children would come up and touch our hands. They seemed startled when I spoke German to them. The adults would ask where I came from in Africa. I would tell them that I was an American from the United States of America. They would ignore my answer and say.

"No, I mean before you went to the United States."

When I explained that I was born in the United States, very often my explanation wasn't accepted. I never understood why they found that so difficult to accept and believe. If I told them that I was an African student going to school in Germany, then they believed me.

Not every German was nice to Americans, especially when they had a few drinks. There was resentment from young German men when American black or white guys were with young German women. Some of the older Germans wanted all Americans to leave Germany.

The Germans would often talk about you when they thought that you didn't understand them. It gave me great pleasure to listen to their conversations. Sometimes I would let them know that I spoke and understood German when it was a benefit for me. Other times, I just kept quiet.

Bobby and Shorty

Bobby was one of my best friends, and we lived in the same building on base. His room was next to my room. We did a lot of things together and enjoyed each other's company. Shorty was also a friend but only out of necessity. Shorty had a car, and he used his car as leverage to maintain friendships. If you were his friend, he would allow you to ride in his car. If he got angry with you, he would leave you stranded. Bobby would joke that if we ever got into a fight in a guesthouse with the Germans, he would take that opportunity to kick Shorty's ass.

Chicken Dinner

One experience that stands out in my mind happened in a German restaurant. We were young men from the United States, living in Europe without a lot of exposure. Our knowledge of culture was limited because we hadn't seen or done many things before coming to Germany.

Bobby and I went to a German restaurant to eat dinner. We had gone there once before, and this time we brought our friend, Shorty with us. The hostess seated us and gave us the menus. While Shorty looked over the menu, Bobby and I had already decided what we wanted to order, so we placed our menus on the table. Noticing this, Shorty said that he would have whatever we were ordering.

This restaurant was very upscale. Each table had a white tablecloth on it with a beautiful flower arrangement in the center. The settings consisted of plates, silverware, glasses, and white cloth napkins. When the waitress came to take our order, we all ordered the chicken dinner, just as before when Bobby and I had eaten there. Each dinner included a large piece of chicken, baked potato, salad, bread roll, and dessert. Except for the dessert, all of the dinner items were served to us at the same time. When we finished eating our dinner, our plates were removed from the table. The waitress returned to our table carrying several small plates and bowls half filled with water with a lemon slice floating on top. She placed the small plates in front of us and set a bowl on each small plate. I asked Bobby if he wanted my lemon soup. He had enjoyed it so much the last time we were at the restaurant. Shorty began to laugh.

"Let me get this straight. Are you telling me that Bobby ate the contents of that bowl the last time you were here?" He asked

I told Shorty that not only did he eat his

soup, he also ate my serving. I described how Bobby took his bread and tore it into little pieces and placed them in the soup and used a spoon to finish eating his soup. At that point Shorty had started to convulse from laughing. We laughed along with Shorty, not knowing why he was laughing. When Shorty regained his composure, he told us that we were really ignorant country people. He explained that the bowls were called finger bowls because they were used to dip your fingers into after eating chicken to remove the grease. Then the bowls would be removed, and our waitress would bring us dessert and place it on the small plates.

Well, we didn't know anything about finger bowls in Arkansas and Mississippi, where Bobby and I came from. We continued laughing after finding out that Bobby had been eating finger bowl water, thinking it was soup. That was the last time we ate there. We were too embarrassed to return to that restaurant.

"Heavy"

I had earned a reputation for being someone who liked to debate and have philosophical discussions about things. In my building, I was considered a pretty good debater. The fellows who lived in by building would call you "heavy" if you expressed opinions about a lot of different topics. A favorite pastime was challenging someone from another part of the base. Living with a bunch of young men, almost everything was turned into a competition. A meeting would be arranged where the "heavy" guys would debate each other. In one of these meetings, I was selected to represent my building. The meetings were held in the base library's conference room.

My supporters would sit or stand on my side of the conference table. The other person's supporters would be on his side of the conference table. We had no rules; we talked about anything and everything. How well you did in the debate depended upon using a lot of so-called big words while speaking with conviction and authority, never showing any weakness or allowing your opponent to out talk you on any topic.

So we began debating the then-current events. Malcolm X and Martin Luther King, the civil rights movement, women's rights, and the Vietnam War were in the news. I was for Malcolm X and women's rights and against the Vietnam War.

My opponent talked about those events and a lot of other nonsense. Sometimes he took my point of view, and other times he argued against his own stated position. We talked around and right past each other for about an hour. I had no idea what he was saying or what he believed, and it was difficult for me to follow his train of thought. So I just threw out stuff that made me seem knowledgeable. When we ended the discussion, everyone on both sides seemed to be satisfied with the results.

I kept my reputation as being an intelligent (heavy) guy. On our way back to our building, I said to one my friends. "What the fuck was he talking about?" He was too heavy for me.

Roommates

During my four-year stay in Germany, I had many roommates. One of them lived with me the entire four years. His name was Manuel. He was a Mexican guy from East LA, California. I should have learned to speak some Spanish over that period of time, but the only thing I learned was, "*Qué pasa?*" ("What's up?" in Spanish).

Another roommate, Donnie, came from an air base in Japan. He was a fifth-degree black belt in karate. His hands were lethal weapons. Donnie was a bad MF. He once showed me how he could kill a person with just one blow. He taught karate classes on base.

After completing each class successfully, you would earn another level and another color belt. Donnie's students would put on demonstrations, showing how to break wood boards in half with their bare hands. Sometimes, they would use bricks in place of wood. Donnie stayed in Germany when his tour of duty was over and opened a karate school.

My jazz-connoisseur roommate Wendell bought a beautiful piece of furniture, a record console, with him to our room. He was a lover of jazz music and had a large record collection. We were one of the very few rooms that had a record console, and we always had nice jazz music playing. That was both good and bad; it was good because the music was nice to hear and bad because all the jazz musicians and jazz lovers hung around in our room. I would come into the room, and there would be four people sitting on my bed listening to music.

When Wendell returned to the United States, the music went with him. While living in the same room, and with his help, I gained some appreciation of jazz music.

Here I am with my roommate Wendell.

One of my favorite roommates, Kelly, lived with us for a full year. Kelly wasn't afraid of anything. He once told me that a dog bit him on the arm, and he became so angry that he grabbed the dog by the leg and bit him right back.

Hypnosis

I was always curious about hypnosis, so I went to the library on the air base and read as much as I could about how to put someone under. I practiced the techniques without using a real subject. When I felt that I was ready, I asked my roommate Kelly if he had ever been hypnotized. He said no and that he didn't believe it was possible for him to be hypnotized, but he would be willing to be my subject. Kelly and I were in the room alone. I didn't want to try this in front of an audience until I had done it at least once. So I asked Kelly to sit in a chair, and I stood in front of him. I used the techniques explained in the books I had read on how to hypnotize someone. After about ten seconds, Kelly was under. I told him he was feeling sleepy, and he closed his eyes and slept. Next, I told him to stand up, turn around, and sit back down, and he did those things. I thought he was just pretending to be hypnotized. So I went further. I asked him to bark like a dog, and Kelly barked. Then I told Kelly to wake up when I clapped my hands. After clapping my hands, I woke him up. Kelly then asked me when I was going to hypnotize him. I told him I had already hypnotized him. He did not believe me.

I was surprised how easy it had been to hypnotize Kelly, so when I had a few people in our room, I asked Kelly if he would be willing to allow me to try hypnotizing him again. He didn't object. So now that I had an audience, I was anxious to show my new skill. I put Kelly under quickly. I did the dog-barking routine, but I want further this time. I told Kelly that he was six years old, and his dog had died. I asked him how did that made him feel. Kelly started to cry in front of all of us in the room. He turned into that six year old right in front of our eyes. The other people in the room felt sorry for Kelly, and they asked me to bring him out from under hypnosis. Before I brought him out from under hypnosis, I had to get him to stop crying. It was very difficult to get Kelly to stop crying. I became frightened and lost my confidence in my ability to wake him.

I told him that he was now twenty-five years old, and his dog was okay. Finally, Kelly stopped crying. I told him that he would not remember anything that had happened and to wake up when I clapped my hands. Kelly woke up as though nothing had happened. The people in the room thought that Kelly and I had played a trick on them. When someone asked Kelly how he had cried so easily without being embarrassed, he answered that he just went along with the gag. After everyone left the room, Kelly asked me why the fellows were talking about him crying. I told him what happened, and again he said he didn't believe me.

I have often thought about that experience and the long-term effect it had on me. I learned a very valuable lesson. You should not play around with human emotions, because you really don't have any control over how a person perceives things that you may take for granted. Kelly trusted me, and I 'didn't show enough respect for his trust. No one should try to manipulate someone's feelings just for the fun of it. The person that you hypnotize may not even be in control of his own emotions. I haven't tried hypnosis lately, so I am a little rusty. Would you like to be my next subject?

A Cold with a Fever

When I went to Germany at eighteen years of age, it was illegal for me to drink liquor. I was given a military ration card that could be used to buy liquor, but I couldn't actually drink it, which doesn't really make sense, but it was that way until I turned twenty-one. I could drink beer in the airman's club but no liquor. They would check your ID in the airman's club sometimes to see if you were underage, but it didn't matter because I didn't drink liquor. The first time I drank was due to my being sick with a cold and fever. One of my friends suggested drinking some cognac. He said it would clear up my cold. We were driving out of town to spend the weekend with our German friend in Saarlouis. It would take about an hour and a half to drive there. On the way, my friend gave me a full bottle (25.4 ounces) of cognac, and suggested that I drink some as we traveled.

When we arrived at our destination, he asked me for the bottle of cognac, and I told him that I had drunk the whole bottle. He said that was impossible and asked me how I was feeling. I said okay and tried to get out of the car, and then it hit me. I was unable to stand up without help. I became drunk and sick on the spot. People were talking to me, but I couldn't respond or feel anything. My brain had shut down. Someone sat me in a chair and left me to sober up. I tried to stand up, but I couldn't move. When I tried to speak, no one seemed to understand what I was saying. Finally, after twelve hours, I begin to regain some of my senses. It felt like I needed to throw up, but nothing was left inside of me. I was actually drunk and sick from Friday night to Monday morning. My friends took turns taking care of me for those three days. In my whole life, I had never been that sick. I was totally dehydrated. Every time I tried to drink some water or anything, I would get drunk and sick all over again. I just wanted to feel normal again. My cold was gone after sobering up; however, I wanted to strangle my friend who had suggested that I drink cognac to cure my cold. That was probably the worst drunk I have ever had. Drinking a fifth of cognac in an hour and a half and living to tell the story became my claim to fame. My friends would say that I drank so much cognac in a short period of time that I had a gnac attack.

Why continue drinking after having such a horrible experience? I don't know, but I continued. On many other occasions, I got drunk from beer and wine. Germany is a drinking country. You can't hardly go anywhere without drinking.

We would go to a guesthouse where they had this glass boot that was two feet tall and as wide at the top as a large beer mug. Shaped just like a cowboy boot but twice as large, it would be passed around the table that seated ten to twelve people, and everyone at the table would take a drink out of the boot, one at a time. It took both hands to hold the boot.

The game started when, the full boot of beer was given to a person to take a drink.

Then the boot would be passed to the next person to take a drink. If the person after you drink the boot empty, then you were responsible for paying for the next boot. This game would continue until everyone was as drunk as possible and still standing.

I remember making a big mistake at a guesthouse after passing the boot around. I had to go to the toilet. Someone gave me directions to the toilet, but in my drunken state I went into the kitchen instead. I was about to pee into the sink when my friend Bobby came in and said.

"NOOO, you're in the wrong place."

And then he took me to the toilet. I was reminded about that incident whenever he wanted to poke fun at me.

I am with Bobby, some German friends (top picture) and with Shorty. (bottom picture)

Agnes

My German friends took me to this village called Roden, close to the city of Saarlouis. We would often go to a guesthouse named after the owner, Agnes. At first appearance it looked like any other guesthouse that we were used to visiting, except the young women waiting the tables were in their late twenties and early thirties. They were older than the other young women that worked in guesthouses.

Normally, guesthouse seating had tables with four chairs and nothing else. Agnes's guesthouse also had that type of seating in the daytime. The place was rearranged differently at night and especially on weekends. Two sliding walls were opened up to reveal what looked like living rooms. They had nice, soft couches and chairs with low tables in front. Candlelit lamps sat on end tables, and beautiful maroon drapes hung in front of the windows.

We went to Agnes's place during the day most of the time, when beer cost less. At night the beer and other drinks would double in price.

Agnes, the owner, looked to be in her middle fifties, was about five feet six inches tall with dark, short hair, and was a little on the heavy side but not fat. When she spoke with you, her voice sounded confident and clear; even though she displayed a motherly type personality toward everyone, you knew that she was the boss.

Her husband Nickolaus was a small man about the same height as Agnes, and his hair was beginning to turn a little gray on the sides, which made him look older than his wife.

Their daughter, young Agnes, was five feet seven inches tall and in her late twenties. Her skin looked as if it was naturally tan all the time. She had a beautiful face with shoulder-length black hair, which complemented her slender figure. You would never guess that she had two children. Her husband Josef was a handsome man who looked about thirty. He was six feet tall with brown hair and a muscular build. He was very friendly and very jealous. When we went to Agnes's guesthouse, I would speak German with her, and she would help me by correcting my German. Everyone working in the guesthouse helped me. They treated me like a family member.

Their home was in the same building as the guesthouse, with a kitchen on the first floor and their bedrooms on the second floor. I was invited to their home one Sunday morning to have breakfast with the whole family. I noticed that the young women who were waitresses also lived with Agnes. They joined us for breakfast. As we sat and had breakfast, Agnes asked me if I could bring them some liquor from the base. Nickolaus said that they would pay me ten times more than it cost me to purchase on base. I happily agreed to their terms.

I brought them liquor every time we visited their guesthouse. Liquor was rationed to servicemen monthly. My allocation was four bottles per month. This turned out to be quite a little profit-making enterprise for me.

On Friday nights, Saturday nights, and Sunday afternoons, the guesthouse was always packed. The living room sections would be opened up to provide additional space for the mostly male customers. The waitresses would remain in the living room with their customers. The men bought expensive bottles of champagne, wine, and shots of liquor for the tables in the rooms. About every hour a male customer would leave the living room with his waitress and go upstairs. She would give him a tour of the bedrooms, and she 'wasn't even a real-estate agent.

Agnes and family were the owners of a

guesthouse that turned into a brothel at night and on weekends. At the same time, the young women waitresses would turn into prostitutes. You could make arrangements to have sex with them for a price. Prostitution was a legal business activity in Germany.

On Saturday and Sunday, it was very difficult to find a parking spot close to Agnes. Their backyard was used for VIP parking. The yard would be filled with expensive German vehicles. Several waitresses would be sitting in the living rooms next to their customers. Young Agnes would also be sitting with the executives. Her section was filled with the wealthiest executives; they bought the most expensive drinks.

On Sundays when we visited the guesthouse, young Agnes would ask me to take Josef (her husband) away for a while to Luxemburg because he was extremely jealous. He could not watch his wife sitting on the coach drinking with other men without saying something to the men. So Agnes paid me in US dollars many times to take him anyplace for several hours.

I almost never had to buy drinks in Agnes's place, because usually the young waitresses and the owners would just bring drinks and leave them on my table. Drinks that had been purchased by the customer seated in their section

About every six months a new group of young women would come from other parts of Europe to work at Agnes's place. Each one of them had a unique appearance or distinctive personality. While in Germany, I never though very much about Agnes's guesthouse also was a brothel. Now when I reflect back on the situation, it was an incredible experience I had at nineteen, selling liquor to the owners of a whorehouse.

Are you wondering if I was ever paid in trade? I will never tell.

Building Confidences

After learning to speak German, my confidence increased tenfold. German was very difficult to learn, and sometimes I wanted to stop and give up, but I kept on making mistakes, and finally the day came, and I was speaking German. Why didn't I quit? Because of my very low-skill job in the motor pool, driving vehicles, I was motivated to continue learning German. The US Air Force hadn't trained me or given me a skill that was usable out of the military. Not wanting to waste four year in the US Air Force without learning something, I decided to attend as much school as possible and get a degree at the expense of the US Air Force. That was my original thinking until I learned to speak German. The language exposed me to so many new real-life adventures that I didn't attend anymore classes. I learned something of value from every contact that was made with the German people and their culture. I was a friend to

Americans who couldn't speak German and a friend of Germans who couldn't speak English. My social life benefited the most from my learning German. Learning helps to build confidence and success.

Chapter Five

Vacation in Scandinavia

While in Germany, I had an opportunity to travel to a lot of different countries. Each country in Europe was different from the other. The culture, the food, the language, and the people were all different. Still the countries were so close together. It would be as if each state in the United States was a different country. Whenever I had time off from work, I traveled to different countries in Europe. My job in the motor pool also allowed me to travel and work at the same time.

Did you know that women outnumber men three to one in Sweden? After reading that in an issue of *Playboy* magazine, my friends and I talked about that article several times, and we really wanted to find out if it was true. I went to the travel agent to get as much information as possible about Sweden.

The research I did was shared with my friends. When we began talking about going to Sweden, five people said that they would like to go. In order to take full advantage of our trip, we decided to take a tour of Scandinavia. The tour cost too much money to pay at one time, so we had to make our payments over several months. When it was time to make the first payment, two people dropped out, leaving me, Bobby and Porcher, just three of us to take the tour. We made payments whenever we had saved enough money. Cities we decided to visit were Copenhagen, Denmark; Stockholm, Goteborg, Sweden; and Oslo, Norway. It took us about a year to pay for the trip that included transportation and housing for two weeks.

The day finally came for us to take that long train ride from Germany to Scandinavia, which was over two thousand miles roundtrip. The train ride would take us a night and a day to reach our destination. The train departed the station at 7:00 p.m. and traveled all night to arrive in Hamburg, Germany, the next morning. This was where the train entered a ferry that had an upper and lower deck. One deck was for cars, and the other deck was for the train. After the train was driven on the ferry, we were allowed to get out of the train and walk around or lounge in chairs on the top deck of the ferry. It took us about an hour to cross the Baltic Sea and dock near Copenhagen, Denmark. We continued on and arrived in Stockholm the next day. Our tour included some boarding at a college dorm. The dorm was empty of students and was used as a hotel during the summer.

We brought lots of liquor with us. At that time, we could buy it for a small amount of money on base, and it was almost like having liquid gold. The Europeans just loved all of our liquor. So we packed up as much liquor as we could carry before we left the air base. After checking in, we hit the road, looking for our three women for every man.

We met a few young Swedish men in a nightclub, hoping they would introduce us to some young Swedish women. We went to a few clubs with them but had no success meeting young women.

We quickly discovered that the Swedes were not very friendly that first night we went out. At first it was kind of shocking when we went into a nightclub to see an entire dance floor filled with beautiful, young women dancing with each other. I had seen young women dancing with each other in Germany a few times but never in large numbers. It happened at every club we went to in Sweden.

It was getting late into the night before I finally got a young woman to dance with me after being rejected several times. As we danced, she asked me if my friends and I were gay. I said no, and then she wanted to know why we were hanging around a bunch of gay Swedish guys.

Then the light went on. Because we were with the gay guys, the young women thought we were also gay and showed no interest in us. If I had read the *Playboy* article in depth, I would have known that the article said the women outnumbered straight men three to one.

Note to self: *remember to always read the complete article in the future.*

After the young women learned we were straight guys, they invited us to an orgy that night. The things that we saw and experienced were shocking. I have forgotten most of the details from that orgy over the years except that I became a little paranoid and suicidal. Need I say more?

Carnival in Stockholm

One evening the three of us went to the Stockholm Carnival in the park. That night, up onstage performing was Louis Armstrong with his orchestra, and they were fantastic. What a nice treat and surprise. It didn't even cost us any money. It was considered a cultural event and was paid for by the Swedish government. There was no seating, but we were able to stand close to the stage. When we moved even closer, it became obvious to the orchestra members performing onstage that we were also American.

I remember someone from the orchestra coming over to us at the edge of the stage. Now I would like to tell you it was Louis Armstrong who came over, but I am not that sure anymore. I am sure what he asked us.

"Where you cats from?"

We told him we were from the US Air Force base in Ramstein, Germany.

"What are you doing here in Stockholm?" He asked.

"We are on vacation," I said.

"Well, I hope you enjoy the show."

After that brief exchange with a member of the orchestra, we became very popular. We had no rejections when we asked young ladies for a dance that night. Now that event is very special to me. At the time, it was just another experience that occurred at random. But it was a unique scene because of the world-famous black jazz musicians onstage performing. While three young black American men were in the audience watching them performance in Stockholm Sweden, in 1965.

Another different experience occurred that summer in Sweden, and that was viewing the midnight sun. During our two weeks, the sun was out most of the time. It was difficult to adjust your sleeping to the daylight. In June the sun began setting at 10:00 p.m., but it wasn't completely dark until midnight. The sun would come back out at about 3:30 a.m. Daylight lasted close to twenty hours.

Goteborg, Sweden

We stayed in Stockholm for half of our vacation. We only had fourteen days vacation from the military. It had taken us a whole day and half just to get to Sweden on the train.

From there we went to Goteborg, the second-largest city in Sweden, which is where they build the largest ships in world. We took a boat tour of the shipyard and watched the ships being built. We spent one night in Goteborg. That night we went to several clubs but finally found a jazz club with a black piano player from South Africa who spoke English. Everyone seemed to know him. When he took a break, he invited us to his table. Beautiful women surrounded him, and we thought we had found the three-women-for-every-man nightclub. We danced with the women and had a good time, and when it was time to leave, the piano player asked us where we were staying. We told him, and he suggested that we come home with him. Our next question to him was if any of the women would be going home with him, and when he said no, we said goodnight and goodbye. We had learned from our experience in Stockholm about the gay men population. We had to go all the way to Sweden to meet our first black South African man who was gay and played American jazz on the piano. What a wonderful world!

Oslo, Norway

Our next stop on the tour was Oslo, Norway. We stayed with a family who rented rooms overnight. After being shown to our rooms, we left our luggage and went out on the town.

A Norwegian theater was showing a new American movie at 10:00 p.m. We went to the movie and got out at midnight. The sun was still high in the sky, and it looked as though it was about 3:00 p.m. The farther north you travel, the longer the days become.

It was too bright to go to bed, so we went to a nightclub. I could not believe the average height of the Norwegian woman. After dancing with one of them, I felt intimated by her height. We left the nightclub at about 2:00 a.m., with the sun going down.

We had a disagreement about the route to take back to the house where we were staying. Confident about the way back, I convinced Bobby to come with me. Porcher went in a different direction. When we got back to the house, Porcher was not there. We waited, expecting him any minute, but after waiting for about fifteen minutes, we went to bed. The next morning at breakfast, Porcher accused us of leaving him behind. He was very upset with us because he had gotten lost.

The sun went down on his way back to the house. He said it turned black outside, and it started to rain. I can only imagine how he must have felt being lost, wet, frightened, and unable to speak the language. He still brings up that incident whenever we reminisce about our tour of Scandinavia.

Copenhagen, Denmark

Our last stop on our way back to Ramstein, Germany, was Copenhagen, Denmark. We did not have enough money for a hotel or meals. Unfortunately for us, before we got to Copenhagen, we ran out of money and liquor. Very hungry and depressed, we just stayed on the train and fought off hunger.

A German family who brought their lunch with them joined us in our train compartment. Shortly after the train got underway, they began eating lunch. We watched them like vultures as they ate lunch. Seeing the looks of starvation on our faces, they offered to share their lunch with us. But not wanting to show our craving for their food, we declined the invitation.

They must have sensed that we were just

being polite in rejecting the food. A bag containing food remained on the seat when they left. What happened after they were no longer in our compartment and out of sight was pure joy. I cannot find the words to describe how we felt eating those scraps of food, except to say that meal will always be one that I will remember and appreciate.

The cost of the Scandinavian tour was well worth the investment. The return on investment has been fifty years worth of storytelling and wonderful memories to share with family and friends. That vacation was one of my best investments.

I am with Bobby (top picture) and Porcher on a ferry that carried our train from Germany to Denmark across the Baltic Sea.

*I am on the ferry from Hamburg, Germany to
Copenhagen, Denmark.*

Chapter Six

Dating Barbara

'Barbara's father was killed in World War II, when she was a baby. Barbara was born during the war in October 1942. She lived with Maria, her mother and Otti, her sister and Patricia, her two-year-old niece, in a small village called Felsberg, (Saarland) Germany. They produce a lot of German wine in the Saarland region. The next-largest city is Saarlouis, located near the French border. Nationalities changed in the area, based of whoever was in power at the time. Sometimes it was France, and other times it was Germany. Barbara's town was in France until 1957, when the citizens were given an opportunity to choose their nationality, and they voted to rejoin West Germany. Barbara's maiden name is French, and she still has relatives living in France who remained French citizens.

When I was nineteen and Barbara was twenty we began seeing each other regularly. Our relationship was just kept friendly for a long time. Nothing serious took place between us until after I had been in Germany for almost two years. Shortly after the Kennedy assassination in 1963, our relationship became more serious than just friends.

I would not describe the beginning of our relationship as love at first sight. Our love for each other grew over time. We began seeing each other every weekend or whenever my job gave me the opportunity to travel through her region on my way to a military base or post.

Waiting to meet Barbara after her work day ended, in the city of Saarlouis, became a normal part of our dating routine. Barbara was a hair stylist, and we would meet at a guest house called the Mexico or the Ice Café after work. We would hold each other's hands, and she would say that my hands were so soft. 'Barbara's hands were not as soft, because she used products with chemical in them while styling hair at her job.

When we were together, time seemed to go by so fast. We talked and danced for a little while, and then Barbara would have to go and catch that last bus to the village of Felsberg. We would go to the bus stop together and wait for her bus. When we saw the bus coming, we would kiss and say goodnight.

Sometimes, Barbara had enough money to pay for a taxi to take her home. She would intentionally miss the bus and stay longer. But then when she got home, she had hell to pay.

Coming home after the last bus arrived, always created tension with Maria, her mother and Otti, her sister. They would be upset with Barbara when she came home later than expected. Life wasn't easy for Barbara at that time.

Wanting to court Barbara the same way it was done back home, I asked her to introduce me to her family. When I asked to meet her mother, she would say that it wasn't a good idea. She thought we might encounter some problems with her family. But I felt whatever objections the family had with our relationship could be overcome in time. Barbara tried to explain how her family would react to her dating a black American man, with the emphasis on "black."

She had no problem with my meeting her Aunt, Maria who was Rosa's mother. Her Aunt Maria always welcomed us into her home.

After I got a car, I would drive Barbara and her cousin Rosa home. I would park my car at least a block away from her Aunt Maria's house, because Barbara was afraid that her mother would see the car with US license tags and put two and two together.

Barbara the Adult

When Barbara turned twenty-one, she had endured enough family conflict and left home for good. She and a friend moved away to another city for a while. Her family sent out a posse to find her. They notified the police that she had run away from home. Barbara was an adult, and there wasn't anything that the police could do about her leaving home. Had her family found out the town where she was working, they would have contacted her job and tried to get her fired. Her mother sent Barbara's paternal uncle to all of Barbara's known friends' homes looking for her. Her family made her life very difficult at that time. Barbara was always a step ahead of the posse. She found a job as a hair stylist in Luxemburg. I visited her in Luxemburg several times. She kept in contact with me through her cousin Rosa. Because she no longer lived at home, we were able to see each other more often, and our relationship just grew stronger. I wanted to marry Barbara and bring her home with me. We talked about marriage, but Barbara was still so afraid of her family and what they might do to us.

While in Germany, I never met Barbara's mother or sister. I did meet her two-year-old niece. Barbara brought Patricia with her once. When I first saw her, she had an ice cream cone in her hand. She was the friendliest member of Barbara's family then and now.

I asked Barbara to marry me, and I gave her an engagement ring in September of 1965. I would be leaving Germany in November and wanted to reassure her that she was coming with me. She had enough time to get her visa and passport in order. We planned to get married in the United States. So many servicemen promised their girlfriends exactly the same thing as I had, but once they were in the United States, the girl never heard from the guy again.

We found out that Barbara was pregnant before I left Germany, so we had a new sense of urgency about arranging for her to come to the United States. It was important that she left Germany before she was showing her pregnancy. We didn't have enough time to get married in Germany or any money for a plane ticket. We didn't even have a place to live in the United States. I couldn't bring her home with me to my 'parents' house in Arkansas. Our marriage in Arkansas was considered a crime in 1965. The law wasn't changed until 1968. Looking back at all of the obstacles we had to overcome, it is unbelievable that we just didn't throw in the towel and quit. Four months before Barbara arrived in the United States, she moved into a hotel near Ramstein Air Force Base. This was shortly before I left for the United States. The hotel bill had been paid for only one month. When the month was over, Barbara found a job as a live-in babysitter in the area. This provided her with a place to live and food but very little money.

I am with my girlfriend, future wife, Barbara.

Becoming a Man in Europe

The Vietnam War and the civil rights movement gained momentum while I was stationed in Germany. During that time, the news we received came from the military newspaper *Stars and Stripes*. The US military TV network also provided news. We had very little information about the day-to-day events in the United States or the rest of the world. We were told only what the military wanted us to know. Some of the most important changes in the history of the United States were taking place in the early 1960s. Our lack of news was good and bad at the same time. It was good because we were unaware of the marches and demonstrations taking place in the United States. So we didn't find it necessary to take sides on any of the issues. That could have led to fights amongst the troops. It was bad because we were not aware of the changes taking place, nor did we have a chance to participate or contribute at the time.

The four years that I spent in the US Air Force in Germany shaped me for the rest of my life. It was very important to my overall development. The US Air Force provided me with the opportunity to go to Germany in the first place. Germany and Europe showed me that my life in the United States had been so limited. Born and growing up in the segregated southern United States, with its lack of respect for human rights, its inequality, and its restrictions had me feeling uncertain, conflicted emotionally, and very unhappy. Germany offered me so much more freedom than I had experienced in the United States. When I left the southern United States in 1962 to go to Germany, I was oblivious about how other people on the planet lived. Exposure to other countries and cultures from the age of eighteen until the age of twenty-two helped to shape me, my beliefs, and my life's future direction.

The happiest time in my life was making discoveries and experiencing firsthand events and new things about my world and me. I had felt like an alien in the delta because of its location, people, culture, prejudices, inequality, and overall environment. I had grown up next to the Mississippi River in Arkansas. Living in Germany, I no longer felt alienated. I had to leave my country, unfortunately, to feel comfortable in my skin.

Back in the USA

When I returned home at twenty-two years of age, I was a different person. My parents had to get to know me all over again. We hadn't spoken or seen each other in four years, so we had a lot to talk about. When I left home at seventeen years of age, marriage to a German girl was inconceivable. My parents were more than a little surprised with my announcement that I was going to marry a German girl as soon as she arrived in the

United States. That announcement wasn't met with a great deal of enthusiasm. Did they have a problem with me marrying a German girl?

I first asked my father what he thought about that, and he said when he was a young man he married the person he wanted to marry and that I should do the same thing. When I talked to my mother, she said she didn't know if it was such a good idea having a mixed marriage. I would not be able to bring my wife home to the South with me. She also said that she felt the children might have some problems with identity. I respected my parents, but I wasn't asking for their permission to get married. I just wanted their good wishes.

I was happy to see my parents again after four years. It was nice to be back in my hometown, if only for a brief period of time after being discharged from the US Air Force. But if I wanted to get my fiancé to the US I had a lot to do. The most important thing was to find a job right away. Before I left Arkansas, my mother and I had a long talk about my intentions, and she said if it would make me happy, I should marry the girl who I loved.

Returning to Detroit, I began to look for work, starting with the Michigan Employment Security Commission (MESC). I took a lot of tests to determine what I was qualified to do. After I completed the testing, I was sent out on job interviews. My first interview was with the National Bank of Detroit. I must have done well on the interview because they offered me a job. They gave me a tour of the bank and showed me where I would begin working. They took me to the lower level of the bank, several stories underground, to the check-processing department. Next, they took me to the vaults where the bills and coins were counted, sorted, and packaged. I was told that all managers started on the lower level and worked their way up to the top. That's where I would start if I took the job in their management-trainee program.

I went home thinking about the offer, but before making a decision, I discussed it with my brother. He wanted to know how much pay they had offered me. I explained that it wasn't very much money to start, but I could work my way to the top. He said the starting pay was much better where he worked. I really needed to make as much money as possible right away. I called the next day to thank the bank and to let them know that I wouldn't be taking the job.

Ford Motor Company

My brother James worked for the Ford Motor Company. He convinced me to consider working for them. They were hiring, and he would recommend me for a job. Ford gave their employees the opportunity to sponsor relatives. On my 'brothers recommendation I secured an interview and went to the Ford employment office to fill out a job application. They gave me a short quiz and asked if I had been tested by the MESC. I informed them that I had, and they called MESC to determine how I had scored on the tests. After they checked my scores, I was hired. I started the following Monday at the Dearborn Engine Plant as an assembly worker. My brother worked at the same plant. I was assigned to work upstairs on the dayshift, and he worked downstairs on the nightshift. So I wouldn't be able to ride to work with him because we worked different shifts.

Monday morning at 6:00 a.m., I caught a city bus that went to the Ford River Rouge Complex. The Dearborn Engine Plant entrance gate was on Miller Road. The bus ride took almost two hours to get to the plant. My shift started at 8:00 a.m. I was the first person at the foreman's podium next to the assembly line. When the foreman arrived, he introduced himself and assigned me to a person to train me for my new job, and that was it. Not even a "Welcome to Ford Motor Company" greeting. Just get to work!

I was glad to have a job with Ford Motor Company that paid twice as much as the bank had offered me to start with them. The benefits the automotive companies provided were better than any other industry. The United Automobile Workers Union (UAW) made sure that their members were well taken care of. My benefits would not start until April 15, 1966, ninety days from my start date. Medical expenses would be covered for my wife and unborn child almost as soon as they arrived in the United States. Barbara was scheduled to come to Detroit by the end of February.

It had taken me only a week after I returned from visiting my parents to find a job at Ford Motor Company. I was living with my brother James and his wife Rose. Now that I had a job, I began to look for a place for us to live.

Barbara arrives in Detroit

Upon being discharged from the US Air Force, I received mustering-out pay and unused vacation pay. All of the money was sent to Barbara for the purchase of her flight to the United States. Speaking with her on the phone to determine if she had received the money, I learned Barbara was having trouble obtaining a six-month visa. So I told her to take a chance and get a three-month visitor's visa. I felt that once she was in the United States and we were married, we could fix the problem with the visa. The next time we spoke, Barbara had obtained the visitor's visa and booked her flight. Now we just had to wait until she arrived in the United States.

I had rented a second-story flat less than a block away from where my brother lived. It was a clean, little place, very nice, and it had two bedrooms, a kitchen, a dining room, and a living room.

A month before Barbara was scheduled to arrive; I spent time after work fixing up the flat. The hardwood floors were sanded and stained. All of the rooms were freshly painted and the windows washed. All the furniture in the flat was obtained from used stores. In the kitchen was a table with two chairs, a gas stove with a missing oven door, and enough dishes for two people. One bedroom was small, and it had enough space for a bed and dresser. The second bedroom, dining room, and living room were not yet furnished. Humble beginnings but enough to get started, and I felt that when Barbara arrived, everything was going to be okay.

The day finally arrived when Barbara was scheduled to be on a plane to the United States. That day had been the most anticipated of my life. I was filled with joy and at the same time frightened. If everything went okay, it would be a great day. But if anything went wrong, it would be catastrophic.

When I received the call that Barbara had gotten though customs in New York, I was thrilled. Now just one more flight and she would be in Detroit with me.

The night that Barbara arrived in Detroit it was snowing very heavily. My friends Orice Dennis and his wife Bernice took me to the airport. It was after 10:00 p.m. before her plane arrived from New York. I was so excited when I first saw her come off the plane. She was looking all around for me, and when she saw me, a smile came over her face.

Five months pregnant, Barbara had successfully hid her pregnancy from the customs and immigration officers and made it safely to Detroit. She had accomplished a very difficult task, and I was so proud of her. Filled with joy, love, and happiness all at once, I was so thrilled to be with Barbara again after three months of not seeing her or being with her.

After we picked Barbara up from the airport, we drove to our flat on the east side of Detroit, where our friends dropped us off. It was after midnight before we got to the flat. Barbara and I talked until she couldn't stay awake any longer. That next day she slept late into the day. I had to go back to work very soon. I tried to arrange things so she wouldn't feel so isolated.

The phone company came to install the phone. Barbara was reluctant to have a phone because she couldn't speak English, but it was a necessity. If she had a problem or wanted something, the phone was the only way of communicating with me or my sister Vicky.

I worked during the day, and Barbara was alone all day. She could not speak English very well, and she was afraid to go outside until I came home. Try to imagine that you are in a foreign country, you are in a house all day alone, you cannot speak the language, and the only person you know who can speak your language in the country is at work all day. What if that person gets into an accident or doesn't come home for some reason? What would you do? Would you be frightened? That was Barbara's predicament.

The phone was installed, and Barbara could contact me on the job if she needed something. From the job, I would call Barbara on every break and talk to her so she didn't feel so alone. She was completely and totally dependent on me. It was a difficult time for both of us. It wasn't long before Barbara got up enough courage to answer phone calls from people other than me. My sister and my sister-in-law would call Barbara and ask her if everything was okay and if she needed something or wanted to go shopping with them, just to get out of the house. They even tried to speak some German with her. Barbara quickly learned enough English to have short conversations.

Married Twice

The week after Barbara arrived; we went to the Wayne County Court House in Detroit and got married. We were married on March 1, 1966. My brother James and his wife Rose gave us a reception after we were married. It was very well attended. A lot of people brought gifts. Most of the people who attended were friends or family members of my sister-in-law, Rose. My older brother Edward and sisters Vicky and Jerry were invited but had reasons that they could not attend.

The party was held in the basement of James's house. Music played on a record player, and people were dancing. James was the bartender, and as he poured the drink he would say.

"Drink up and eat as much as you like. It's all paid for."

Everyone wanted to meet Barbara and welcome her to the family. They tried to talk to her, so I spent most of the night interpreting for friends and family.

Even though we had been legally married at the courthouse, my sister-in-law Rose suggested that we do it again, but this time in front of a minister. One of Rose's family members was the pastor of a church. It was decided that Barbara and I would be married again by the pastor at his home on Wednesday of the next week. So we were married twice.

I am still grateful for the help that I received from James and Rose. Life for us would have been so much more difficult if it were not for their help. They allowed me to live with them until Barbara arrived. They let us use their car to go shopping and for other necessities. We had a standing invitation for dinner anytime we wanted to join them. When we needed money, they loaned it to us. They were two of the kindest people I have ever known.

Immigration and Naturalization Service (INS)

We applied immediately for permanent-residence status (a green card) for Barbara. We waited a week before we got an appointment with the Immigration and Naturalization Service (INS). Barbara had entered the United States on a three-month visitor's visa. We had very little time to fix her status. In our first interview with the INS, most of the questions were directed to Barbara. I was asked to interpret for the INS interviewer because Barbara didn't understand English, and he didn't understand German. The first question to Barbara was.

"Why did you lie on your application for a visa? You applied for a three-month visitor's visa when you knew that you were coming to the United States to get married and not return to Germany."

I told Barbara what he had said.

"What are we going to tell him?" She asked.

I told him that Barbara said that she hadn't lied. If she could not get a green card, she would go back to Germany within the three months. Then he asked me if I would return with her.

"Yes, of course I will return with her. She is going to have our baby." I said.

"Why didn't you get married in Germany?" He asked.

"We didn't have enough time because the paperwork in the military took to long." I said.

He asked me, to ask Barbara if I had ever abused her. After telling Barbara what he had asked.

"Is he stupid?" she asked.

"She said, 'NEVER!" I told him

He wanted to know if I had a job, how much I earned a week, if we had any money saved, and if we had our own place. The questioning went on like that for an hour. Finally he said that we must let the INS know if we changed our address within the first year.

About thirty days later, Barbara received a green card in the mail. What a relief, but that wasn't the last time a person from the INS would interrogate us.

Double-dipping Doctor

We had to find a doctor to provide prenatal care for Barbara. My sister Vicky recommended a clinic that was about two miles from where we lived. We didn't have any health insurance yet. It took ninety days from the first day of employment at Ford Motor Company before we could qualify for health insurance. I hadn't worked ninety days, so we had to pay each time we visited the doctor. The clinic wanted the money paid in advance, and we didn't have enough. (Poor people get screwed all of the time.) I'll explain. The doctor had a finance company with an office in his clinic. When we told his receptionist we didn't have enough money to pay the full amount, she directed us to the finance company. We took a copy of the bill with us. The finance person said that after reviewing the bill, she could loan us the money, but we would have to pay interest on the balance each month until it was paid off. After we signed the loan documents, the doctor saw Barbara the same day. This doctor was double dipping by charging for his services and charging interest on the payments we made to him. I wonder if things like that still happen.

Money for Nothing

We didn't own a car, so at 6:00 a.m. every morning, someone picked me up to take me to work. After paying for rent, food, utilities, and the doctor's care for Barbara, very little money was left over. We didn't have enough money to buy a car or pay for gasoline and automobile insurance, but we saved enough for a down payment on new furniture. We purchased a living room set, dining room set, television, kitchen table with chairs, lamp tables with lamps, and window drapes at Sears. We put all of the furniture on lay-away and paid it off in three months. The total cost of everything was $795

After we got a TV, Barbara watched every day. She learned enough English from watching to help her find and select groceries when we went shopping. Sometimes she just looked at the pictures on the labels and picked up the wrong thing. I would check the items to make sure she had selected correctly. When I found something that shouldn't be in the basket, I put the items back on the shelves. Selections such as rug shampoo instead of hair shampoo, dental crème instead of toothpaste, and canned tuna for cats instead of tuna fish in a can for human consumption are just a few examples. Those experiences are always good for a laugh when we talk about things that happened at the beginning of our marriage.

Do-rag

What is a do-rag and how is it used? Ask almost any black person that question, and it would be answered correctly. That's something we just know about and take for granted. If you are not familiar with a do-rag, it is usually a piece of sheer cloth used to cover the head. 'It's worn to help produce waves in the hair or retain and preserve straightened or processed hair. A hair relaxer is often used first to produce the desired results before the do-rag is used.

When my wife first came to the United States, she often observed black men wearing do-rags. She didn't know how they were used or why. But she believed she understood the reasons. One day as we sat on the bus, several young black men got on wearing do-rags. Barbara said she felt so sorry for them. Not seeing anything about them that made me feel sorry for them, I wanted to know to whom Barbara was referring.

"Those poor young men who just got on the bus." She said.

Looking at them carefully this time, I still didn't find anything different about them.

"Why do you feel so sorry for them?" I asked.

"Because their heads are all bandaged; they must have been in a terrible accident and have major head injuries." She said.

I explained to her that they 'didn't have bandages on their heads. Next, I tried to help her understand what a do-rag was and how it was used. Explaining why it was used became more of a challenge. At first she 'didn't believe me because styling hair was her occupation in Germany. She had gone to school and became a certified, licensed hair stylist. She 'hadn't been taught anything about do-rags. That was understandable because there were very few black people in Germany.

You might expect when questions about do-rags are asked in the United States, most people would know what they are and why they are worn. I think 'you'll be very surprised. Other than black people, most Americans don't know what a do-rag is and how it is used. If you don't believe me, just ask anyone you know.

Family and Friends

Some good friends we had known in Germany returned to the United States a few months before we arrived in Detroit. They lived in Gary, Indiana, and had kept in contact with us. Soon after Barbara got to Detroit, we went to Gary on the train to visit them. Barbara was so happy to see her girlfriend from Germany.

We spent the weekend with the family. On our way back to Detroit, Barbara seemed a little sad. She would be alone again, not having anyone to speak German with except me.

Barbara was expecting the baby in May, and we didn't have a car. So we made arrangements with family and friends to pick Barbara up if she had to go to the hospital. I was home weekends, and my brother would let me have his car just in case I needed to take Barbara to the hospital. We went shopping whenever we had the car. As luck would have it, I was at home for the Memorial Day holiday when Barbara went unto labor. I took her to the hospital and stayed with her until she had the baby. We had a beautiful baby boy whom we named Darnell. Barbara has a rare blood type, RH negative. Because of her blood type, it could have created complications for the baby. So Barbara and the baby remained in the hospital an extra day for observation. The day she came home with the baby was truly a wonderful day.

Barbara's cousin, Linda lived in Chicago with her husband, Shelton and their two-year-old son, Benedict. She had come to Detroit with her son a day before Barbara went into the hospital to help Barbara with the baby. After Barbara came home, her cousin was very helpful, teaching us how to do things new parents needed to know about taking care of an infant. Her cousin had planned to stay with us for a few months, and we were glad to have her stay. Shelton came to visit, and after discussing employment opportunities, he decided to stay and look for work. He was an electrician by trade. He applied for work with all of the automobile companies. Chrysler Corporation hired him on the spot. He and his family lived with us in Detroit until they found an apartment and never returned to Chicago.

Benedict was very rambunctious at the age of two, and he would run all over the living room and dining room. The noise that his little footsteps made must have disturbed the owner of the flat who lived downstairs. She would yell at us if he walked across the room. She would knock on the ceiling and scream like a mad person. Everything was okay with her until Barbara's cousin's family moved in with us. After a week, she asked if the little boy and his mother would be living with us. The landlord told me that they would have to leave or pay additional rent. We couldn't have any guests or visitors. She would screen all of our visitors. I thought she was out of her mind. We could not do anything in our flat. This woman would scream in the morning and at night for no reason. We believed she must have been deranged.

We begin looking for a house to purchase to move away from this crazy woman. My sister, Vicky had seen a house for sale on her street a block away from where she lived. The house was on the east side of Detroit on a street named Lemay. It had a living room, dining room, a kitchen, two bedrooms, and one bathroom. There was a shower in the basement. You gained access to the garage through the alley.

We made an offer on the house that was accepted. Using a (Veterans Administration) VA loan, we paid $9,500 for our small, little house.

During that first year of our marriage, Barbara came to the United States and got her green card, we had a baby, we bought new furniture, and after living in a rented flat for six months, we purchased our first house and moved into it.

Once we got our own place, we started getting visits from all of our friends who came to the United States from Europe. We were so proud to have our own place. Our old landlord did us a big favor by annoying us and forcing us to move. That's how we got started owning real estate. We had plenty of visitors that year. I was twenty-three years old, and Barbara was twenty-four.

I had another friend whom I knew from Germany. He and his wife lived in Chicago. We wanted to spend some time with them as well. We took the baby on the road in our recently purchased used car. Of course, this car broke down on the way. It kept running hot and stopping. It took us over six hours to get to Gary, Indiana, where we slept overnight with our other friends. The next morning, we continued on to Chicago. Our friends were very happy to see us. They lived with his mother and father in this small house. We had to sleep on the floor with the baby. During that time, we didn't seem to mind where we slept. We slept on floors, couches, and car seats. It didn't matter because we were young.

Our lives went on like that for a while, with friends visiting and Barbara gradually learning English, and I begin teaching her how to drive a car. Vicky helped her learn how to cook soul food. Barbara is a very good cook, and that includes cooking soul food.

We ran out of money all of the time. Barbara took all of the money out of her, German pension plan, which certainly came in handy. I borrowed money from my brother and his wife at other times. We were just borrowing, as we needed help at times. I remember my brother Edward would not loan me any money, and he told me I had to I ask his wife, Lilly, my sister-in-law. Lilly would loan me money and tell me.

"Don't tell your brother."

Most of the time we borrowed what we needed and always paid it back on time. I never asked my older sister Jerry, to loan me money, but I did borrow from my younger sister Vicky. We made it the best way we could. I don't know how we would have made it without family.

This was our first house in Detroit in 1966.

Chapter Seven

Dearborn Engine Plant

My brother had been my sponsor for the job at Ford Motor Company. Once again my family came to the rescue.

By now I was just another person on the assembly line whom the tour guide pointed to when he explained something about the construction of an engine. I always looked at the tour groups to see if I recognized some of my friends or family taking the tour of the giant Ford Dearborn River Rouge Complex. Over 250,000 people took the tour per year, and I was part of the tourist attraction.

The assembly line that I worked on was about a mile in length, and it ran contentiously. Sixty to ninety engines were produced per hour, depending on how much available inventory was on hand. The engine block began production as just a piece of nonfunctional material, and by the end of the assembly-line process, it was a finished engine ready to be installed in a car. Each worker on the assembly line inserted or attached some part to the block. The crankshaft was installed in the block first and the pistons next. Then the block came to my work location, and our job was to check to make sure that the pistons had been installed properly.

When no problems were found, we marked inside the engine block with our identifying character to show it had passed inspection. Three people worked at my location, and each of us had his own character to identify who inspected the engine. My character was a check mark. Someone else used a zero, and the other person used x as his character. This way management would know who had inspected the engine if something went wrong.

Hot Test

After the engine was completely assembled, it was started and ran for a few minutes. That process was called the hot test. It was the last thing done on the assembly line before the engine was installed into a car.

One day, our foreman, the shift supervisor, and the plant manager came toward us at a rapid pace as if something catastrophic had happened. The foreman commanded one of my fellow workers to come with him. He and the other managers walked away quickly. The worker had been abruptly removed from the assembly line, leaving just the two of us to pick up his workload. We could only speculate about what problem had caused all of management to get involved.

The worker returned in fifteen minutes, but before I had a chance to ask what had happened, my foreman beckoned and asked me to come with him. We walked all the way to the end of the assembly line, where the hot test was done. Several people were standing around a disassembled engine. My foreman told me to go and take a look at what happened when an engine throws a rod. The piston had come unattached or broke off from the crankshaft, and it blew a hole through the engine block. It was similar to when a broken bone comes through the skin.

The foreman explained how dangerous it was for the people running the hot test when an engine throws a rod. He told me how much money the company loses when a piston blows through an engine block. The greatest losses were from downtime in the hot-test area. Engines just piled up until the hot test was back on line. They had found the character of my fellow worker in the engine block, and if it happened again, he would be fired.

What if that had been my check mark in the engine block? I could have been fired. We couldn't afford to lose healthcare benefits with a baby coming in a few months. In order to make sure that I wasn't ever in jeopardy of losing my job because one of the engines that I had inspected failed the hot test, I did something that I am ashamed about today. I stopped putting my check mark character in the engine blocks that I inspected. I used the two characters of my fellow workers. I would mark a zero or x character in the engine block, alternating between the two characters but never using my check mark. Did anymore engines blow up on future hot tests? Yes, but never one with a check mark.

The GI Bill

Initially, I was glad to have a job at Ford Motor Company, but as time passed, I begin to dislike working in the plant. It was very noisy and smelled like oil. The oil scent got in all of your clothes and seemed to penetrate your skin. Taking a shower didn't get rid of the plant smell from your body.

The air conditioner in the plant seemed to never put out enough cold air in the summer months. In the winter months, it was always too hot in the plant. The assembly line never stopped, and you had to stand on your feet the entire shift. Tempers would flare up, and fights would break out inside the plant and in the parking lot. I begin to dread going to work. I had to find another job before someone got angry with me and wanted to fight.

Being unskilled limited opportunities for other employment. I begin to think about my future and how soon I could get out of the plant.

On our breaks, we were allowed to smoke in the plant. At that time, I smoked a pack of cigarettes a day. While opening a book of matches to light my cigarette, I noticed an ad inside the matchbook cover about a vocational technical school called the Automation Institute. The ad said, "Become skilled in data processing. Learn to program and operate computers." I had no knowledge of what computer programming was all about. It just sounded impressive to say that you were involved with computers.

I would have to find out if the school was approved for the GI Bill, which provided government money to former servicemen for school, based on the number of years they had spent in the military. I qualified for thirty-six months of education under the GI Bill.

In Germany, I had earned one year of college credits from the University of Maryland, and I had planned to attend Wayne State University in Detroit on the GI Bill. When I visited a counselor on campus, I asked if computer programming was offered at Wayne State University. He said yes, through the mathematics department, but before taking any computer-programming courses, I would have to complete my second year of college. Computer programming wasn't offered until junior year. He asked if I planned on going to school fulltime. I told him that was not an option at the time because I needed to work for a while. He discouraged me from attending Wayne State University if I couldn't go fulltime. He suggested that I look into attending vocational technical school or community college to accommodate my work schedule.

That visit helped me to make up my mind, and I enrolled at the Automation Institute for computer programming. It would take a year to complete the classes, attending school on Saturdays and two nights during the week. It wasn't easy working and going to school. This was the worst time for us.

Barbara still needed me to help her with the language. She hadn't learned how to drive yet. I had to drive her and the baby everyplace. One good thing, we were both young and had lots of energy. Just thinking about how much we had to do back then make me tired now.

That school year went by very slowly,

but it finally ended, and I graduated with a certificate in data processing from the Automation Institute. I took two weeks vacation from Ford Motor Company to look for a data-processing job. On the Friday before I left for vacation, at quitting time, I said my goodbyes to the people whom I had worked with, side by side, over the last eighteen months. Some of them didn't believe my saying goodbye made sense because they expected me back after two weeks. They told me I would be back working with them within the month. What I did next confirmed to my fellow workers that I had certainly lost my mind. With them looking on, I went up to the foreman, extended my hand, and said.

"It's been nice working for you. I just came to say goodbye, and that you'll never see me again."

He looked at me a little perplexed, smiled, and said.

"I'll see you in two weeks."

I shook his hand, turned, and walked away, and that was the last time he ever saw me.

New Opportunity

After walking out of the plant that Friday, I wasn't sure if what I said to the foreman would come true. My reason for telling the foreman goodbye and that he would never see me again was my way of burning all my bridges behind me. I wanted to make it very difficult and to embarrassing for me to return to the plant.

I went home and started to look for jobs in the newspaper. Three days of that first week went by without me finding an opportunity. On the fourth day of the week, I saw one potential opportunity in the newspaper.

NCR Corporation was looking for

computer programmers. I called about the job and set up an appointment with the personnel director for 4:00 p.m. on Friday, a week from the day that I had gone on vacation.

The interview took place as scheduled and lasted forty-five minutes with the personnel director. Then he asked me to take a test. This test was given to all NCR computer programmers. He said I could take the test that day or come back on Monday at 8:00 a.m. and take it. I don't know why, but I decided to take the test that day. It was 4:45 p.m. on a Friday when I started the test. After reviewing a few questions, I decided not to take the test. I went back to the personnel director's office and told him that I hadn't really begun the test yet and that I would like to come in on Monday. He said that would be okay. Had I continued taking that test, and failed to pass it. My life would be different today.

The test was called the E51 aptitude test for electronic data-processing programmers.

That weekend I went to the library on the Wayne State University Campus and inquired about the E51 test. I was successful and found a lot of information about taking the exam and an example of the E51 test. I practiced taking several different programmers' tests, including the sample E51 test. I was at the library half of the day.

I returned to the NCR office on Monday morning and took the test. The test had only eleven questions on it. I completed the test in an hour. After checking my answers, the personnel director told me that I had answered seven questions correctly, and that was considered a passing score. He took me to meet the person who would be my manager if they hired me. I met with the manager, and he asked me how soon I could come to work if they offered me the job. I told him, "Next week." He said they would get back to me within the week to let me know if I got the job.

It was Monday, the second week of my

vacation. I had one job opportunity and one interview without an offer. I was running out of time. How could I go back to Ford Motor Company after making my declaration to the foreman and saying goodbye to so many people in the plant? It was now Wednesday, and I hadn't heard anything from NCR Corporation. I wanted to call them, but I didn't want to seem desperate. On Thursday morning, I received a call from the personnel director, asking if I could start working for NCR Corporation on Monday of the next week. I was so happy that I didn't have to go back to Ford Motor Company. When the personnel director asked me if I had any questions, I didn't even ask how much my starting pay would be or any questions about benefits. Do you realize how many things could have gone wrong in the two weeks that I was on vacation? Everything had to go right for me to make that declaration to the foreman come true. The power of positive thinking was surely at work that time.

The 1967 Detroit Riot

Off in the distance, you could hear the sound of automatic weapons firing late into the night. It reminded me of Fourth of July firecrackers all going off at the same time. The noise would be so loud and then suddenly stop. Silence for a few minutes, and it would start all over again. Each subsequent time, it would seem to get louder. That is where the similarity with the Fourth of July ended.

Detroit was burning, and there weren't enough policemen, firemen, or equipment to put out all of the fires and arrest all of the looters. We heard the sound of fire trucks and police sirens and someone speaking on loudspeakers. The smell of smoke from the fires that had been set all over the city left you wondering how long it would be before the worst of the riots would reach our side of town.

Things had gotten so out of control, and the Detroit police could not contain the riots.

The Michigan National Guard had been activated but wasn't able to make a difference. There was talk of calling up reserve military personal. When the riots broke out in July of 1967, my greatest fear was that I would be called up for active military duty as a reservist. I was eligible to be called until November 1967, two years from the date of my discharge from the US Air Force.

The mayor of Detroit asked for help from the federal government. The Eighty-second Airborne Division soldiers were sent to Detroit to stop the rioting. This was the same group of soldiers who had been fighting in Vietnam. It was dangerous, scary, and unbelievable. These soldiers patrolled every street in Detroit.

I had spent four years in the US Air Force, and during that time I hadn't seen any combat, but back in the city of Detroit, I was living in a combat zone. As the soldiers walked past our houses, they were offered something cold to drink. They had been told not to get into discussions with the citizens and to keep moving.

The entire city was under a curfew. Everyone was asked to stay put until further notice. You were allowed to go places in the daytime, but you could not travel after dark. Things didn't calm down for a solid week. Not before forty-three deaths, eleven hundred injuries, and over seven thousand arrests had occurred.

Two significant events were scheduled to happen in our lives the week of the riots. On Monday of that week, I was supposed to start a new job working for NCR Corporation, and my sister-in-law and her girlfriend were to come from Germany to visit us in the United States for the very first time. Barbara hadn't seen her sister since she left home two years earlier, and I hadn't ever met my sister-in-law. Because of the riots, both events had been postponed for a week. That next Monday I went to my new job, and Otti, my sister-in-law and her friend arrived from Montreal Canada, where their airline had been redirected the week before because of the riots in Detroit. Otti was glad to see Barbara and her new nephew, Darnell.

We spent the rest of her stay getting to know each other. I must have left a favorable impression on my sister-in-law because after she returned home, we were all invited to come to Germany for a visit to Barbara's home. Later that same year Barbara and Darnell went to Germany, but I stayed behind and began working at my new job.

Since that first meeting with Otti, our bond has just grown stronger. We are truly a close family. Otti has been and continues to be a wonderful sister-in-law.

Chapter Eight

New Career

The first day at my new job was exciting for me because I didn't have to go to a place that smelled like oil, was noisy, and had no windows. The NCR building was on West Grand Boulevard in what was called the New Center Area near General Motors World Headquarters. It was a three-story building with equipment and demonstration rooms on the first floor, and the sales department was on the second floor. The service department, computer room, and an auditorium that held three hundred people were on the third floor.

I had earned more money at Ford Motor Company. My starting pay with NCR Corporation was much less, but I was doing what I enjoyed. NCR Corporation hired me as a system engineer/computer programmer. My job was setting up data-processing equipment in the customers' offices and training their people how to operate the equipment. I was assigned to a sales team, working with the customers of that sales team.

The first person whom I worked with was a senior account manager name, Les Wolf. I was his system engineer. After we had worked together for a while, he showed me his commissions check for equipment that I had just trained his customer to operate. The commission check was more money than I earned all year. I was inspired and motivated to try selling. I asked the district sales manager, John Brennan if I could work in the sales department. He said no, that he didn't believe I would make a good salesperson, so I continued to work as a systems engineer, but I inquired about becoming a salesperson often.

The branch library in our building kept all the products and services manufactured by NCR Corporation. It was a pretty extensive library that had, conservatively, five thousand books and other documents. I begin my reading with the A's and went all the way through to the Z's in a period of about nine months. I studied everything in the library, because I wanted to know as much as possible about the products and services.

NCR introduced a new data-processing product to the market. It was called the NCR 735, and it was a key-to-tape machine. This was a product that allowed the operator to input data from a keyboard directly to tape. Up until that time, all information that was input to computers was captured on a punch card using key-punch machines. The punch-card data would be read into the computer through a card reader attached to the computer. This was how most information was input into computers until the 1970s. Key to tape was a much more efficient and less expensive way to capture information and get it processed quicker.

My job was to train the operators how to use the equipment. I must have trained hundreds of operators on this equipment. The government, banks and Fortune 500 companies were the primary users of these machines. I did a lot of training at night because data-capture departments worked overnight. Whole rooms full of women operated the equipment. If they still had questions or needed help, after being trained, they would call me anytime, mostly late at night, and sometimes at 3:00 a.m. I am sure if my wife might have been suspicious with those women calling me at all hours of the night. But she never said anything about the calls.

I kept requesting to go into sales until I was allowed to enter NCR's sales training program eighteen months from my start date.

The NCR sales training program was known as one of the best in the data-processing industry. My training took place at newly constructed facilities near NCR Corporate

Headquarters in Dayton, Ohio. NCR Sugar Camp was the name of the campus where the training was held.

Training took place in three stages, each stage taking about three weeks to complete. After the each stage, you would return to your district sales branch. A sales quota was assigned to you that had to be achieved before you were allowed to return to Sugar Camp for more training. The overall training took a year if you were successful at each stage.

Upon completion of sales training, you were assigned to a senior account manager as a junior sales trainee and given a quota. You would remain in that position until obtaining your sales quota the senior account manager recommended you for promotion to account manager. At that point, you were allowed to work on your own.

After completing my sales training with three other sales trainees in our district branch;

the senior account managers were fighting over which one of them they would take on their team.

No one was fighting to work with me. I can only guess at the reasons. No one wanted to work with me, so the branch manager offered a senior account manager extra commission to take me on his sales team. When I got my first sale, it was on equipment that paid a bonus. The account manager could not believe that I had sold that product. He seemed to be very upset about my sale and joked that he should take all the commission from me. He could have taken it if he has wanted too. I had no leverage. So I said.

"Why don't we just split the bonus, and I will keep my commission?"

I paid him off just to keep my basic sales commission. I didn't mind doing it because I needed his recommendation to get promoted. After making my quota on his team, I was reassigned to another senior account manager as a junior salesman.

The only product I sold as a sales specialist was the new key-to-tape data-processing equipment because of my experience as a system engineer working with that product. The commission was excellent for each product sold. Under this new senior account manager, I was able to learn quickly. Within six months, I become independent and was on my own as a new account manager.

After successfully completing the sales training program, I was promoted to account manager in 1970. I was now in a position as an account manager to build my very own sales team by taking on new junior sales representatives to train.

At the beginning of my sales career, the company reorganized by lines of business: financial, retail, commercial/industrial, and educational/government. My decision was to select educational/government as the area in which to continue my sales career. It was an area that most people really did not like. I believed my best chance for success was do jobs that other people were unwilling to take on. Doing things that other people would rather not tackle became a theme in my career.

Century Point Club (CPC)

Before beginning to build a sales team, I had to prove myself as a successful account manager. I qualified for the Century Point Club (CPC) my very first year of eligibility. CPC was for account managers who obtained 100 percent of their objectives. All of the salespeople who qualified for CPC would be given an all-expenses-paid trip to the annual sales convention. The first CPC sales convention I attended was held in Hollywood, Florida.

I was a rare sight at CPC. Maybe there were other black salespeople there. But I didn't see any others.

Data processing and computers were a new industry. I was extremely fortunate to get involved with computer sales. The next three years I made CPC. My career was off to a good start.

Our compensation plan was salary plus commission, with the most money coming from commissions. The salary wasn't very large, but if you sold the right combination of equipment, you could do well. The first thing I learned was how to evaluate the compensation plan to make sure I was able to optimize my income. It didn't take long for me to determine how to make more money than normal. The products that had incentive on them were what I concentrated on selling.

The reason for incentives or additional commission on some products was because they were more difficult to sell. Other times, we were behind on our quota, and the branch provided incentives to get us back on quota. Sometimes, it was because a newer model was replacing the products. It didn't matter to me what the reasons were. I just focused on selling the highest-commissioned products.

Being Vice President

After earning CPC three years in a row, Bob Dodds the regional vice president in the Detroit region took me under his wings and became my mentor. I had an opportunity to spend a lot of time with him, and we would make calls together. I was always impressed with how he commanded attention whenever he walked into a room. By working with him, I got a chance to observe a true professional. After witnessing how smooth he was on a sales call, I once told him.

"I wish I was a vice president."

He asked me why.

"When the receptionist says that the vice president from NCR is here; you are shown so much more respect." I said.

"On the next sales call, you can be the vice president. I'll be the salesman." He said.

He wanted me to know that respect had nothing to do with titles but with the person. That example made a lasting impression on me. Because of his teaching, I started to see myself differently.

Whenever a sales opportunity presented itself, he would call me into his office and tell me that we would be working together. That meant I did most of the work. This time, I would be working with him on Ford Motor Company.

Signing in at the reception desk in the lobby of the Ford Motor Company World Headquarters building, I thought about working on the assembly line just a few years earlier. Now I was going to a conference room at Ford Headquarters with the NCR regional vice president to be introduced to the Ford Dealers Communication Service Team.

I was assigned as the person responsible for current and future NCR product sales and implementation to the Ford dealers. The vice president introduced me to the Ford team as the person with the authority to request whatever help I needed to get the job done. He stressed that he would also be available to the Ford team and me whenever we requested his involvement. That job assignment became a wonderful learning experience and helped me to develop into a more confident salesman.

NCR met with the Ford Dealers Communication Service Team once per week. We would review the performance of our communications equipment in all of Ford's dealerships. The meetings were held to sort out any differences in the performance numbers.

When our numbers agreed or were not that different, we would have a short meeting. When the numbers didn't agree, we would have to determine who was at fault and why. NCR had guaranteed Ford 99 percent uptime. When the NCR equipment didn't meet the performance target, the Ford Dealers Communication Services Team would deduct an agreed-upon dollar amount from the monthly rental payment.

The Ford team would never take responsibility for the downtime that their dealerships caused. The team always blamed NCR for any downtime. They loved beating up on NCR. That meant they loved to beat up on me.

In each meeting, four Ford team members would be seated on one side on the conference table, and I was seated on the other side. We would successfully negotiate our differences most of the time. However, on one particular occasion, I must have irritated the

Ford team leader. He expressed dissatisfaction with my performance and asked me to bring the regional vice president to our next meeting.

In that next meeting, Bob Dodds, the regional vice president was with me, and we sat together on the same side of the conference table. The Ford team was seated on the other side. The Ford team leader was an Englishman with a superior-than-thou attitude. He asked me to review our information. Everyone listened as I went through our performance for the month. Just before I finished presenting our numbers, the Englishman said in his most annoying, unpleasant English tone.

"Your numbers are rubbish."

When he suggested that we were lying about our numbers, the regional vice president stood up and said.

"Let's go. We don't have to stay here and be insulted."

As we were about to stand up to leave, the Englishman jumped up and pointed his finger across the conference table in the direction of the regional vice president and said.

"We are not done with you yet."

The regional vice president removed his eyeglasses, threw them on the table, and said to the Englishman.

"Take your fucking finger out of my face before I come across this table and kick your fucking ass."

The vice president, a former US Marine, was very well-known in NCR circles as someone who liked a good old-fashioned bar brawl. The Englishman quickly sat back down as I closed my briefcase and walked out the conference room. I didn't know what I really would have done if the vice president had started a fight with our largest customer.

We left the building, and on our drive back to our office, Bob Dodds, the vice president apologized to me for his behavior. In none of my future meetings with the Ford team did anyone ever ask me to bring the regional vice president with me again.

I am being congratulated for making CPC. Bob Dodds (top left) Bob Lapinski (top right) John Curtis (bottom right)

Growth Years

My career with NCR Corporation put me in contact with some of the most important and influential business people in the automotive industry and in the United States. Over two years, my earning improved enough for us to consider buying a larger house.

In 1970, we listed our house for $14,600, and it sold for that price within four months. We had paid $9,500 for the house, earning a profit of $5,100, less expenses. With the help of my brother Edward, we found a larger house on the west side of Detroit one street over from his house. The house we purchased in 1970 cost $25,000 and was located just two blocks away from my cousin, Sherman's house on the same street. It was near west seven mile road and far away from where my sister, Vicky lived on the east side of Detroit.

The next year, Barbara became pregnant with our second child. We had been married five years. Barbara went to the hospital to have the baby a few days before Christmas.

Our Christmas gift that year was a beautiful baby girl who came just in time to be claimed as a tax exemption. Christine was born in December 1971. Barbara was able to come home after Christine was born, but our baby girl had to remain in the hospital for treatment and observation for incompatibility jaundice. That has something to do with the RH blood factor, when the baby's blood is different from the mother's blood. Our baby was given blood transfusions and kept under a light for several days before we could bring her home.

Barbara's mother had come to the United States to be with her before and after Christine was born. This was the first time I had met Barbara's mother face to face, but over the years we had talked on the phone and resolved a lot of issues. By now, all was forgiven, and I had a normal mother-in-law relationship. Barbara's mother and I visited the hospital daily to check on Christine. Our primary concern now was the health of our baby girl. The doctors kept her in the hospital for a week, until she was no longer in danger. When we brought her home, we were all relieved and very happy that she was healthy.

Chapter Nine

Good Advice

"As a young man, knowing what I know now, I would have invested in income property."

That was the unsolicited advice from Joe Decoute, my new regional vice president. He didn't talk to me very much about NCR Corporation. We spoke mostly about real estate investing.

"You'll never become rich working at NCR. You can make a good living, but if you want to make a lot of money, invest in income property."

Rumor had it that Joe was a very wealthy man. He once told me that he had everyone fooled about how rich he was. He said.

"That's my wife's money."

Joe had talked to me about investing in real estate and how it helped him shelter his income. He told me about the money he was making from his real estate investments, and he spoke about it over and over. Eventually, I became interested and started reading about real estate. I even paid five hundred dollars for a weekend seminar on real estate investing. That training would become helpful when we found something to invest in, now that I was earning larger commissions. Investing in real estate could help me keep more money by not having to pay so much in income tax. That became our goal, and we begin looking for income property.

Income Property

Our first exposure to income-property investing was through two young aggressive real estate salesmen who drove a big, long, black Cadillac limousine. They drove us around and showed us real estate all over Detroit.

What they showed us was either in a bad location or too large and expensive. We begin looking for buildings on our own, and after several months we found an apartment complex that we liked on west seven mile road, near lasher road in Detroit, that was for sale. Unfortunately, we could not get the two young men involved who had been working with us, because the buildings were listed exclusively with another agency.

The complex had three apartment buildings connected together that covered the entire block. The apartments were built out of a light-gray brick with gray shingle covering the roofs. Each building had two stories with its own address and entrances. The buildings looked new, but they were seven years old. Twenty-eight apartments were in three different buildings. The west-end and east-end buildings both had nine one-bedroom apartments each. The middle building had ten two-bedroom apartments.

We decided to take a chance and make an offer and see what would happen. This would be a good opportunity for us to get into real estate investing. The agents presented our offer to the owners, and we waited for an answer. After we made the offer, we couldn't sleep. The thought of us losing all of our savings had begun to cause some doubt in our minds. We kept asking each other what was the worst thing that could happen. We were getting cold feet. Before we could back out of the deal, the agency contacted us to let us know that our offer had been accepted.

We signed the agreement, and a closing date was scheduled for the next week. We were either too stupid or too courageous to stop the closing from happening. On May 10, 1976, we closed on our first income-property investment, but it wouldn't be our last.

Crest Management Company

We were in our early thirties, younger than most of our tenants in the buildings. So we kept our ownership and our relationship concealed.

The complex was called Crest Apartments. We used the DBA (doing business as) Crest Management Company as our business name. We also took on aliases. I was called Gary Butler the maintenance man, and Barbara changed her name to Pat Rupp. She was the property manager responsible for renting the apartments and the direct contact at the management company for the tenants. No one in the building knew we were married or that we owned the apartment buildings.

One of the things we did immediately was notify all of the tenants in writing that the apartment building had new owners and new property-management. We introduced Pat Rupp as the property manager and Gary Butler as the maintenance man. We installed a separate business phone in our home for Crest Apartments. In the letter, we asked the tenants to send their checks to the address of the post office box number that we had rented. We told them to contact us at the business phone number if they needed to get in touch with someone from the management company.

Now the real work began; we had to eliminate the resident property-manager position so we could rent out her unit, collect past-due rents, evict non paying tenants, raise rents at the end of expired leases, fill vacancies, advertise apartments for rent, review applications, clean and paint all empty apartments, clean hallways, wash windows, make repairs in apartments as required, and cut the grass in front of the buildings. The apartment buildings consumed us. We had very little time for anything else.

Barbara's first job was to tell the resident property manager that she was no longer employed and that she had to pay rent or move. She was given a week to comply. This went over like a lead balloon. The old resident manager had no intentions of giving up her job. She called our home, telling us to fire the skinny woman with the foreign accent. Barbara left her alone until the week was over.

Barbara went back into the building with an eviction notice to give to the old resident manager, because she hadn't moved or made an attempt to pay. The old resident manager had no respect for Barbara as a property manager. She told Barbara that she didn't have to pay, and she picked up a broom and chased Barbara out of the building with the broom in hand. Barbara became very upset because she couldn't go into her own building without being threatened. Barbara went to the nearest police station and told the police what had happened.

The next time Barbara returned with the eviction notice, she had a policeman with her. The policeman stood just out of sight when

Barbara approached the old resident manager. Again she began cursing and threatening Barbara, but then the policeman revealed himself, and Barbara was able to serve her with eviction papers.

This woman did not go quietly, and she had to be forcibly removed from the apartment by orders of the sheriff's department. All of her belongings were put outside on the street.

Hypocrites

Barbara's next challenge was to try to collect rent from the past-due tenants or have them evicted. After that was accomplished, she advertised for new tenants. The neighborhood was not yet integrated, and all of the people in the buildings were white tenants. Some of them had been in the building since it was built seven years earlier.

Barbara was about to integrate the building with the first black female tenant.

After showing the apartment to the future tenant, she was approached by a number of older tenants who were not so subtle in showing their blatant prejudice. They told Barbara that if she rented the apartment to the black female, they would move and take all of the other tenants with them. Barbara reminded them that it was against the law to discriminate. They didn't care. These were the same old white ladies who went to church every Sunday and were very strong believers in God.

The same ladies always complimented me on how well I spoke English for a maintenance man. When they had problems in their apartments, they welcomed me without showing any signs of prejudice at my presence. When I did work in their apartments, they would often give me tips. Sometimes, my son would come with me to cut the grass on weekends, and they would give him money for ice cream. I will never understand human nature.

The first black female tenant who moved into the building worked for the post office. She would carry packages for the old ladies to the post office and bring them their mail, so she was accepted. The next black tenant was a young man who worked for the city of Detroit in the data-processing department. One other black female school teacher also became a tenant. They were all professional, respectable people with good jobs. After Barbara put three black tenants in the buildings, the complaints increased. The young man played his music too loud, someone parked in someone else's spot, and too many guests were coming and going. The business phone was filled with recorded messages with complaints about the new tenants. Barbara answered all of the messages, saying that we would take of the complaints. In a few months, things quieted down. We received fewer complaints over time, and no one moved out because black tenants were residents in the buildings.

The Boss Lady

The maintenance man's job was to fix minor problems in the apartments and oversee the repairs when outside contractors were used for the more serious work. One of the tenants had a problem with a leaky faucet on the kitchen sink. That was a job for Gary the maintenance man. I fixed the faucet, but it took me some time to repair it. The tenant thanked me when I left the apartment. The very next day when Barbara was in the building, she asked the tenant if everything had been repaired. The tenant complained that it took a long time for me to fix the leak. I was in the hallway vacuuming when Barbara abruptly told me to come into the tenant's apartment. Barbara said with authority.

"Gary, come in here. Why did it take you so long to get around to fixing that leak?"

I was caught off guard, so I just looked at Barbara. I thought Barbara wants to show who was boss. Then I asked the tenant.

"Is the faucet still leaking?"

"No, it's not leaking. I just told Pat that it took you a long time to fix it." She said.

"Yes, it took me longer than normal." I said.

Sensing that she may have gotten me into trouble with my boss, the tenant said.

"It's no big deal."

Then Barbara said to the tenant.

"If you continue to have problems with the leak, maybe we will have to get someone else to fix it."

Then she said to me.

"Gary, I will talk to you later, but check that leak again before you leave."

After Barbara left the apartment the tenant said.

"Gary, I am so sorry if I got you into trouble. How can you work for that bitch?"

"You just have to get to know her. She's not so bad." I said.

Then I left that building to vacuum the hallways in my favorite building, where all of the young tenants lived. The smell of marijuana would be so strong sometimes in that building, I would get high by the time I finished vacuuming. The young tenants would always invite me in for a beer or something to drink.

After Barbara had reprimanded me about fixing the leaky faucet, I headed to my favorite building, hoping it would smell of marijuana or that maybe someone would invite me in for a drink.

Crest Apartments was our first income
property purchased 1976 in Detroit.

Chapter Ten

Moved to the Suburbs

My sales career had taken off, giving me the opportunity to earn more money than ever before. As one of the top NCR salesmen in the country, I was about to receive the largest commission check of my life.

We sold our house in Detroit. With the money from the commission check, we made a down payment on a house in a nice, quiet neighborhood in the suburbs in February 1977. Darnell was eleven, and Christine was six years old. We moved to improve our environment. The school system in the suburbs was better than the system in Detroit. Our new house was located on a ravine lot with a running stream at the bottom of it. The lot was almost an acre, plenty of land for the children to play.

Promotion to District Manager

One morning I received a totally unexpected call from the regional vice president's office. His secretary asked me to come to Chicago, where the regional office was located. She said that the vice president wanted to meet with me. I asked her if she knew the nature of the meeting. She said that she didn't know. He had only told her to book me a flight to Chicago as soon as possible. On my way to Chicago, I begin to speculate about the reason for the meeting while trying to keep an open mind.

After arriving in Chicago, I went directly to the regional office and met with the regional vice president. The vice president thanked me for coming and told me that an opportunity for district manager was opening up in Detroit, and NCR Corporation was offering the job to me. The vice president said that he needed to know my answer by the end of the day. I asked about pay and reminded him that I was earning more money than most district managers. He said that the compensation plan was about to change, and I wouldn't be able to earn the same amount of money that I had earned as a salesman. I thanked him for the opportunity and told him that I would think about it on my way back to Detroit. The meeting took all of fifteen minutes.

On my way back to Detroit, a lot of things went through my mind. I knew that if I accepted the job, I would be the only black district manager in our sales division in the United States. I stopped myself from over thinking that situation. I was a successful salesman, and advancement was a reward for my success.

My credentials were stronger than most other salesmen whom had been promoted to district manager. After some analysis, I decided to take the job, and I told my wife that I had been offered a promotion to district manager in Detroit and that I was going to accept it. She was very excited and happy about the news. I next called the regional vice president and told him that I would take the job. That was just one of the many opportunities that would be offered to me over my long career with NCR Corporation.

A Little Success

Success to me is setting and achieving goals. Becoming successful requires hard work, with a lot of luck and some well-thought-out risk taking. Do you want to know what it feels like to achieve a little success? It feels great!

In 1978, ten years after leaving Ford Motor Company, I was promoted to district manager in Detroit. This promotion was a great opportunity for me to excel and accomplish greater success. I would have to focus on my new job, so we decided to sell the apartment buildings. We had taken a chance on an investment that could have caused us financial hardship for a very long time, had we failed. But on August 18, 1979, after almost three years of ownership, we sold the apartment buildings for a nice profit. Keeping more money from my earnings and paying less in income tax were our goals, and they had been accomplished with that purchase. The investment in the apartment buildings established a tax shelter that lasted far beyond anything we had planned. It helped us to obtain the knowledge and experience so that we could continue to investing in real estate. Over the years, we have been very successful with our income-property investments.

Growing up on Welfare

I will never forget the word "Commodities." My father would go to the county's food-distribution site to pick up our family's share of government commodities. That's what it was called when I was in elementary school. It was not called food stamps. You couldn't hide your poverty back then, and it was out there for everyone to see. You had to stand in line to claim your portions of food. Sometimes, the line was so long that it would curve around the corner of the block. It was a reminder that you couldn't even feed your loved ones without the help of the government. It was embarrassing and humiliating for most people to stand in that line. The only consolation was that almost every family in town was in the same line as your family member. Even though most families received assistance, the children would make jokes and tease each other about eating commodity cheese. Once each month, my father went to pick up various items: sugar, powered milk, flour, butter, canned meat, and yes, commodity cheese. Almost every family in Arkansas received some assistance from the government in the 1950s.

My parents also received Aid to Dependent Children (ADC) money for my care.

In order to receive aid, you had to live below the poverty line. During the time that I was on welfare, a social worker would visit our house every six months. The worker would spend time questioning my parents about how they had spent the money on me. The social worker would speak to me alone, away from my parents. She had a long list of questions that she asked me. The questions were mostly about how the ADC was spent on food, clothing, and shelter. I always resented being put in a position to report on my parents. The ADC checks stopped when I turned sixteen years old.

One of the first things I did after joining the US Air Force was to set up an allotment to my parents. At that time, the military would match your contribution if you could prove that your mother and father were dependent on you. My contribution to the allotment was fifty dollars per month, and the military contributed forty-five dollars, for a total allotment to my parents of ninety-five dollars per month. This must have been very difficult for my father, not being able to provide for his family and having to accept help from the government and his youngest child.

My parents wouldn't have anything to be embarrassed or feel ashamed about now. Their children have paid more than enough in taxes to repay for all of the assistance received from the government over the years.

Thanks, Mama and Daddy

At the age of fifteen, I told my mother and father that I was agnostic. Their reactions were a little different. My father asked me to speak with a deacon from his church. My mother said that I should pray, but I explained that she was the one who believed in God, so she should pray for me to acquire understanding. Telling them that I wasn't convinced and uncertain about God's existence was like coming out of the closet back then. I am sure they were hurt and disappointment with my confession. But I always tried to be open and honest with my parents.

After a year in Germany, I remember writing my mother and father, thanking them for allowing me the opportunity to make decisions at an early age and to live with the consequences. What I had observed about a lot of the servicemen was how easily they were influenced by others. I had a mind of my own, and whenever someone tried to talk me into doing something that I didn't want to do, I just refused.

The influence of the peer group could be overwhelming if you were not strong. Regardless of how much they badgered and ridiculed me, I would always stand my ground for things that I felt were right for me. I didn't know at first where those feelings and strengths were coming from, until I took some time to reflect. They were coming from the values that my parents had taught me. Grateful for the foundation that had been established, with their parenting; I was able to sort out what worked for me.

Having the freedom to think for myself at a young age helped me to develop my own feelings about things. My parents allowed me to express my opinion without trying to force me to come around to their way of thinking. They were in their early forties when I was born and had already raised five children. I received the benefit of their experience. Feeling equipped to handle almost any situation; I thank them for allowing me to be myself.

Here I am with my wife, Barbara.

Thankful Strother

ABOUT THE AUTHOR

Thankful Strother, born in 1943, graduated from high school and joined the US Air Force in 1961. He was stationed in Germany for four years. There he learned to speak German and met his wife Barbara. They married in 1966. They have two adult children.

Thankful Strother had a thirty-five-year career in computers and telecommunications. He retired in 2003. He and his wife live in California and they just celebrated forty-six years of marriage. Now he enjoys visiting the ocean daily, where he watches and listens to the waves while observing nature. In his retirement, he has accomplished his goal to write a book about his early life.

Alien in the Delta is that book.

28738428R00140

Made in the USA
Lexington, KY
29 December 2013